THE VYNE

Hampshire

Maurice Howard

National Trust

Acknowledgements

The major objects within the collection were accepted by HM Government in lieu of Inheritance Tax and allocated to the National Trust for display at The Vyne, 1958.

The National Trust wishes to thank the Victoria & Albert Museum and the Museums and Galleries Commission for the generous partial grant aid in acquiring the pair of Sèvres vases which form the garniture of the Further Drawing Room; and the Heritage Lottery Fund for supporting the recent restoration of the Chapel.

This account of The Vyne has been written by Dr Maurice Howard, who would like to thank the following: Rosalys Coope for all her patient, collaborative work on the Tudor house; the Duke of Rutland for permission to consult the 1541 inventory of the house at Belvoir Castle; the Sandys family for access to the seventeenth-century family double-portrait and much other help on the history of the family; Francis Chute for help with illustrations and the family tree; Christopher Currie for his invaluable survey of the estate, commissioned by the National Trust; Nicholas Cooper for expert advice on the building; Michael Archer and David Gaimster for help with the glass and textiles; Clive Wainwright for advice on the furniture; Charles Tracy on the woodwork. Finally, great thanks to Edward Wilson, archaeologist at the house during the 1997–8 repairs, whose conclusions about the structure and scale of the earlier house will form the basis of further publications. The tour section has been written by Cathal Moore, formerly Assistant Historic Buildings Representative responsible for the house, with picture entries compiled by Oliver Garnett from notes by Alastair Laing.

Photographs: British Architectural Library/RIBA p. 50; Francis Chute p. 63; Courtauld Institute of Art p. 49; Maurice Howard p. 45; Lewis Walpole Library, Farmington, CT p. 58; National Trust pp. 19, 44, 51, 59, 62; NT/Richard Holtumm front cover; National Trust Images: pp. 21, 40, 41, 55, T. Davidson p. 54, Mark Fiennes p. 22, John Hammond pp. 9, 18, 29, 30, Angelo Hornak p. 34, Nadia Mackenzie pp. 11, 13, 24, 26, 32, Geoff Morgan p. 7, James Mortimer pp. 1, 5, 8, 12, 15, 17, 23, 33, 38, 43, 57, Derick E. Witty pp. 6, 16, 25, 27, 35, 36, 47, 53, 56, 60, back cover; Victoria & Albert Museum Picture Library p. 48; Edward Wilson p. 46.

First published in Great Britain in 1998 by the National Trust

© 1998 The National Trust

Revised 2000, 2002, 2008, 2010; reprinted 2004, 2005, 2012, 2013, 2015

Registered charity no. 205846

ISBN 978-1-84359-022-4

Designed by James Shurmer

Phototypeset in Monotype Bembo Series 270
by Intraspan Ltd, Smallfield, Surrey (SG1332)

Printed by Park Lane Press, Corsham
for National Trust (Enterprises) Ltd, Heelis, Kemble Drive, Swindon SN2 2NA
on Cocoon Silk made from 100% recycled paper

(*Front cover*) The Chapel

(*Title-page*) The winged goat crest of William Sandys; from the Oak Gallery panelling

(*Back cover*) Catherine of Aragon; from the early sixteenth-century stained glass in the Chapel

CONTENTS

THE VYNE

THE VYNE is a house with a long history which has been respected and imaginatively reinterpreted by a succession of owners over the last five centuries.

Like many medieval foundations, it stands on low-lying ground and near water – the Shir brook, which was transformed into a spectacular lake setting for the north front in the eighteenth century. The irregular pattern of brickwork, ranging in colour from pale to deep red, reveals how much the exterior has been altered, with symmetrical sash-windows imposed on an earlier, more random arrangement. On the north front, a portico stands with classical correctness equidistant between two towers, but the façade itself is unsymmetrical, as a wing containing a Tudor Gothic chapel extends from it to the east.

What we see today is only a fragment of a much larger Tudor house, which was created in the early sixteenth century from a number of free-standing medieval buildings by William, 1st Lord Sandys, Henry VIII's Lord Chamberlain, who died in 1540. The visitor who stands on the portico side, facing the huge expanse of lawn, is looking over an area once covered by a series of Tudor courtyards. However, the portrait of Henry VIII in the Chapel stained glass and the royal arms in the Oak Gallery panelling still offer potent reminders of the era when The Vyne was the 'power house' of a great Tudor courtier, who entertained the King three times here.

The wealth and power of the Sandys family declined during the next hundred years and was finally broken by the Civil War. In 1653 the estate was sold to Chaloner Chute, Speaker of the House of Commons in the last Commonwealth parliament. He reduced and modernised the house, commissioning Inigo Jones's most talented pupil, John Webb, to add the classical portico, the first of its kind on an English country house. But Chute died in 1659, probably before he could complete his scheme, and little seems to have been done to the house during the next hundred years.

Speaker Chute's great-grandson, John Chute, who inherited The Vyne in 1754, was a close friend of Horace Walpole and helped to design the influential Gothic Revival interiors of Walpole's villa at Strawberry Hill in Twickenham. Chute was a talented architect, but also a cautious antiquarian who appreciated the complex history of his ancient home. Although he devised various Gothic schemes for The Vyne in keeping with its Tudor origins, his real inspiration was the era of Speaker Chute, whom he commemorated by creating the Tomb Chamber. The Vyne is still full of the mementoes that Chute brought back from his long Grand Tour of Italy in the 1740s.

In the early nineteenth century The Vyne entered a period of benign neglect, which helped to preserve its ancient interiors. When a more active owner, William Wiggett Chute, took up residence in 1842, he modernised the services, but it is typical of the family that he fitted out his new Library upstairs with a seventeenth-century chimneypiece and woodwork. His son, who was named after Speaker Chute, wrote A History of The Vyne (1888), which is one of the most scholarly late nineteenth-century country-house histories. And in the same spirit, the historian's son, Sir Charles Chute, 1st Bt, gave the house, its contents, and estate to the National Trust in 1956.

Since 1994, the National Trust has been reordering the house on the basis of research into the family papers. In 1996, The Vyne was closed for extensive repairs in the course of which several rooms were partially redecorated and arranged, two bedrooms were furnished and opened to visitors for the first time, and the eighteenth-century mural paintings were restored to the Chapel. The aim is to restore a sense of continuity and domesticity.

(Opposite) The Staircase Hall

TOUR OF THE HOUSE

The Exterior

THE SOUTH FRONT

The south front became the main entrance to the house during the eighteenth century, when John Chute, who lived here from 1754 to 1776, built a new central staircase. When The Vyne was first built in the early sixteenth century, this was probably the private side of a substantially bigger house. Recent investigation suggests that the present service wing to the right is seventeenth-century. Much Tudor brickwork survives with its 'diaper work' (blackened brick headers and stretchers creating a pattern of lozenge shapes). As on the west and north fronts, the wider Tudor windows that were

replaced in the seventeenth century can still be made out through breaks in the diaper pattern. In the centre there was a tower, which was replaced in the mid-nineteenth century by the present gable and two-storey porch, bearing the Chute coat of arms (three swords barways).

The skyline would originally have been more interesting, with battlements, or possibly a series of small gables, and taller chimneys. The projections in the angles where the wings meet the main block now serve as porches. They are decorated with the crests of Chute (a hand in a gauntlet grasping a broken sword) and of Wiggett (a griffin's head holding in its beak an ear of wheat). The pair of

The north front

stone eagles flanking the central doorway were a gift from Horace Walpole to John Chute in 1745. The bay windows in the wings were added by Wiggett Chute in the mid-nineteenth century.

THE WEST FRONT

The west front contains two galleries: the early sixteenth-century Oak Gallery on the upper floor and the Stone Gallery, which took its present form in the eighteenth century, on the lower. A roof survey has shown that the tower at the north end was built later than the wing itself, probably in the seventeenth century. Recent excavation has revealed footings of what may have been an earlier, polygonal tower in front of this façade.

(Opposite) The south front in the mid-nineteenth century, before the two-storey porch and the gable had been added to the centre of the façade by William Wiggett Chute

THE NORTH FRONT

The north front was essentially created in the seventeenth century, when the tower and range to the right was built to match earlier Tudor work to the left, all then provided with sash-windows. The façade is dominated by the portico added by John Webb for Chaloner Chute in the 1650s. Chute also removed substantial buildings stretching down to the water's edge; these formed the base court of the Tudor house, approached by a bridge, the remains of which are submerged in the lake. The portico columns and pilasters are of brick, rendered with stucco. Their Corinthian capitals are of Burford stone, as is the coat of arms of the Chute family in the pediment, which was carved by Edward Marshall. The pediment is painted wood.

The battlements were placed on the ranges between the towers during the nineteenth century, although there were probably already battlements or gables here in Tudor times. The wing at the east end, beyond the tower, contains the Ante-Chapel and Chapel, which were screened by trees until the nineteenth century, when the blind windows were inserted in the Chapel. Some of the stone cresting to the Chapel may be original; it contains the Sandys arms with the Garter William achieved in 1518.

THE EAST FRONT

In the Tudor period there was another entrance to the house on this side. Much of the east front is concealed by a once-private garden, but the Tomb Chamber, added by John Chute to the south side of the Chapel and unfinished at his death in 1776, can be seen. This side of the house was the domestic service wing, containing the kitchen from at least the mid-seventeenth century. Upstairs, a schoolroom and further bedrooms for the household were created by Wiggett Chute in the nineteenth century.

The Interior

THE STAIRCASE HALL
AND STAIRCASE LANDINGS

The space occupied by the present Staircase Hall was probably occupied by an open hall in the Sandys house. The 1541 inventory refers to a staircase, which was probably located at the north end of the Vestibule. Edward Marshall's accounts (1654) refers to paving work in the 'hall before the Chapel and Cellar'.

John Chute created the present staircase between 1769 and 1771. In 1755 Horace Walpole had recommended a staircase of four flights, but, characteristically, Chute delayed carrying out the work for some time, while he sketched a large number of alternative Gothic, chinoiserie and classical designs. *The Topographer* of May 1789 described what he eventually devised as 'the Grecian theatric staircase'. It takes maximum scenic advantage of the awkwardly long and narrow space (44 by 18 feet), and, when seen from the foot of the stairs, creates an extraordinary perspectival illusion of architectural depth. The quality of the carved wood columns and balusters (which are versions of the seventeenth-century balustrade under the central window of the north front), and of the ceiling mouldings and plaster soffits is very fine, but, unfortunately, the identities of the craftsmen responsible are unknown.

The only later alterations have been the introduction of the lobby to the south entrance and the removal of the stone floor to the south terrace in 1842 by Wiggett Chute, who substituted softwood boards. The present decorative scheme, devised c.1960 by the 8th Duke of Wellington and John

The Staircase Hall

Fowler, was partially inspired by scrapes attempting to reveal John Chute's 1770s colour scheme. However, recent paint analysis has revealed that the 1960 interpretation of the paint scheme is misleading. The columns, frieze and ceiling were painted white, while the flat of the wall was painted sky blue, suggesting that the intention was to create a setting of ruinous classical architecture.

PICTURES

MARTHA CHUTE (d. 1888)
*The Main Hall, c.*1860

NORTH LANDING, EAST WALL:

After ? HENDRICK VAN STEENWIJK II (c.1580–1648)
St Peter's release from Prison
Bought by Wiggett Chute in 1847.

NORTH WALL, RIGHT OF WINDOW:

ENGLISH, c.1720
Francis Chute (1696–1745)
Elder brother of John Chute. A barrister and friend of scholars.

NORTH WALL, LEFT OF WINDOW:

ENGLISH, *c.*1720
Anthony Chute, MP (1691–1754)
He inserted the sash-windows in the north front and
bought furniture from Vile and Cobb for the house.
He was succeeded by his younger brother, John.

SOUTH LANDING, WEST WALL:

VICENTE GINER (active *c.*1680)
Preparing for Market or *Architectural Setting with
Figures*

EAST WALL:

PETER VAN BREDAEL (1629–1719)
Market Scene set among Antique Ruins

FURNITURE

The pair of mahogany card tables, *c.*1765, probably by
France and Bradburne, was fitted into its present
position between the pilasters by Wiggett Chute,
*c.*1845.

A group of six hall-chairs, mahogany, *c.*1765. The
backrests are painted with the Chute arms, three
swords barways. Two chairs are displayed in the
Vestibule.

SCULPTURE

ON STAIRCASE NEWELS:

Mid-eighteenth-century Italian marble busts of the
Emperors Antoninus and Caligula.

In 1754 an 'Egyptian figure' was inventoried in the
house, and in 1776 and 1842 was listed in the lobby
staircase and Stone Hall. This is the green schist
figure of Rameses IV, King of the XXth Dynasty
(reigned 1161–55 BC), which was sold to the British
Museum in 1956 and of which the National Trust
has obtained a cast.

Climb the stairs to the first floor.

THE LIBRARY

In 1754 this was called the Wrought Bedchamber
and in 1776 was furnished with the two lacquer
cabinets to be seen in the Further Drawing Room.
The present room is largely a nineteenth-century
creation by Wiggett Chute. After 1842 he introduced the library shelves, using a cornice from the

The Library

family pew in the parish church. He also installed the woodwork for the ceiling from the North Bedroom, brought panelling for the walls from the other rooms, and replaced the floor.

CHIMNEYPIECE

The chimneypiece, taken from the old Tapestry Room, was probably designed by John Webb and carved by Edward Marshall *c*.1660. The engaged columnar supports of the mantel shelf, in the form of stylised palm trees and the crossed palm fronds of the lintel directly relate to Webb's later designs, particularly that for the bed alcove of the King's Bedchamber at Greenwich Palace.

PICTURES

OVER DOOR (FACING):

After Sir GODFREY KNELLER (*c*.1646/9–1723)
John Locke (1632–1704)
Philosopher.

FIREPLACE WALL, LEFT:

Manner of Sir ANTHONY VAN DYCK (1599–1641)
Dorothy North, Lady Dacre, later Mrs Chaloner Chute (1605–98)
Speaker Chute's second wife.

OVER FIREPLACE:

ENGLISH, *c*.1600
? *Margaret Fiennes, Baroness Dacre* (d. 1610–11) *and her husband, Samson Lennard* (d. 1615)
Once thought to be Speaker Chute's grandparents, Arthur and Elizabeth Chute, but more likely to be ancestors of his second wife, Dorothy, Lady Dacre.

FIREPLACE WALL, RIGHT:

ENGLISH, *c*.1640
Chaloner Chute, the Speaker (*c*.1595–1659)
'A Man of great wit and stately carriage of himself', according to Roger North. He bought The Vyne in 1653 and commissioned John Webb to add the portico. He was elected Speaker of the House of Commons shortly before his death.

OVER DOOR (TO STAIRS):

After Sir GODFREY KNELLER (*c*.1646/9–1723)
Sir Isaac Newton (1642–1727)
The father of modern science and mathematics.

WINDOW WALL:

A framed and illuminated pedigree of the Cufaude family.

SCULPTURE

ABOVE BOOKCASES:

The plaster busts, with three small plaster figures, were bought by Wiggett for £14 in July 1845 and are of Cicero, Dryden, Prior, Locke, Homer, Shakespeare, Milton, Goldsmith and Johnson. A bust of Walter Scott was acquired separately. Busts of famous writers were favourite library furnishings.

FURNITURE

WINDOW WALL:

The two giltwood pier-glasses are English, *c*.1755.

The pair of Buhl pedestal cabinets of ebonised pear wood with brass inlay is English *c*.1840. The mounts and decoration of brass inlay were loosely inspired by the designs of André-Charles Boulle (1642–1732).

CENTRE:

The pair of globes with maps printed in 1818 is English, purchased by Wiggett Chute.

The six side-chairs and two armchairs of carved pine are English, *c*.1870 in seventeenth-century style with later upholstery.

IN GLAZED CASE:

A gold Roman ring, inscribed in Latin: 'O Senicianus, may you live in God.' It was found near Silchester. The inscription suggests a Christian owner.

THE LITTLE TAPESTRY ROOM

In 1754 this small room was the 'closet adjoining the Green Damask Bedchamber' (the present Tapestry Room). A white flower-pattern wallpaper which survives behind the bookcases was put up early in the nineteenth century.

TAPESTRY

The fragmentary tapestry is Flemish, *c*.1720, and depicts the story of Dido and Aeneas. It was moved here by Wiggett Chute after 1842.

The Tapestry Room

THE TAPESTRY ROOM

PICTURE

Late seventeenth-century illuminated family tree of the Brocas family, owners of The Vyne between 1420 and 1488.

FURNITURE

The pair of walnut and partial gilt and upholstered seat furniture, c.1710, is part of a set more fully described in the Tapestry Room.

CERAMICS

The Imari ware plate is Japanese, *c.*1670, on a partially gilt walnut stand, English *c.*1830.

By 1754 this room had become the Green Damask Bedchamber. In the early nineteenth century Elizabeth Chute was using it as her morning-room. The fitted dwarf bookcases were added by her husband at the same period. Wiggett Chute made substantial changes after 1842, when he turned it into a billiard-room. He also installed here, with additions, the chimneypiece he had removed from the Dining Parlour. The ceiling joinery (also with nineteenth-century additions) came from the former school-room.

CERAMICS

Around the room is arranged a large group of principally Chinese Export wares.

The dish and mug enamelled with the Chute coat of arms, Chinese, *famille verte, c.*1785. The dish was found in Norfolk in 1911, and shortly thereafter returned to the Chutes of The Vyne. These two pieces once formed part of a Chinese Export punch set consisting of punch bowls, mugs and dishes, now dispersed. It was probably commissioned by Thomas Lobb or William John Chute.

ON THE CABINET ON STAND:

The Dehua or *blanc-de-chine Dogs of Fo* is Chinese, *c.*1700.

TEXTILES

The group of chinoiserie tapestries, made of wool and silk is English, Soho Factory, under the direction of John Vanderbank, Chief Arras Worker of the Great Wardrobe (1689–1727), *c.*1720. Edward Chute, grandson of the famous 'Speaker', may have commissioned this group of hangings and these are the tapestries described as furnishing the North Bedroom at the time of the 1754 inventory. The tapestry panels were cut down in the middle of the nineteenth century when they were moved to their present location. The subject of the tapestries, which is described as Chinese actually draws on Persian and Indian imagery. By placing the figures on what would have been a black background the intended effect must have been that of Oriental lacquer.

The pair of mahogany stools is English, *c.*1750, upholstered in needlework by Laura, Lady Chute (d.1959), who was inspired by the tapestries.

PICTURE

OVER DOOR:

JOHANN HEINRICH MÜNTZ (1727–98)
An Italian Landscape with a River and Classical Ruins

FURNITURE

The suite of settees and back stools with slip seats, upholstered backs and seats, the frames of partially gilt walnut, is English, *c.*1720. The backrests of both settees, which were originally the same shape as the back stools, were altered to their present, lower shape during the nineteenth century, and is probably the set in the Oak Gallery in 1776, when it was described as having silver and crimson harateen covers.

The marquetry cabinet on a walnut stand is English, *c.*1675–85.

THE OAK GALLERY

The Oak Gallery is one of the very few long galleries surviving from the first half of the sixteenth century and the most richly decorated. The splendid galleries in Henry VIII's and Cardinal Wolsey's palaces at Whitehall and Hampton Court have disappeared, and contemporary examples that do survive all lack The Vyne's wealth of heraldic carving. Close to the royal apartments, the Oak Gallery was meant to be a place of display.

The linenfold panelling is decorated with the royal arms flanked by Sandys's arms and crests in medallions

The Oak Gallery

William Sandys installed the panelling here. It was an ambitious scheme, as comparable rooms in contemporary courtier houses were generally hung with tapestries or painted cloth. It must have been executed between about 1518 (when Sandys received his Order of the Garter) and 1526 (the date of the separation of Henry VIII and Catherine of Aragon) and possibly in 1521–2, when Sandys was employing craftsmen at The Vyne.

In the seventeenth century the window openings were narrowed and increased in number, which must have necessitated altering the panelling.

In 1755 Horace Walpole recommended that the room be 'finished at the ends with carved wainscot'. This was not carried out, although John Chute added considerably to the furnishings, introducing many more pictures, including the six full-length portraits in black and gilt frames. By *c.*1776–89, sixteen portraits hung here, including perhaps pictures from Pickenham Hall, Norfolk, added by Thomas Lobb Chute. In 1780 Mrs Lybbe Powys described: 'Two hung galleries, one full of whole length portraits, in the gallery library are many portfolios of the finest prints' (which in the nine-

teenth century were used to decorate the Print Room on the ground floor). By 1842 eighteen pictures were hanging here.

The panelling was probably covered with the present thin layer of gesso and brown paint in the early nineteenth century. Between 1842 and 1860 Wiggett created the bay window at the south end of the room, installed a new floor, altered the doors at the north end, and had to repair panels damaged by damp. He also considered removing the paint from the panelling, but was prevented from doing so by the cost and difficulty. However, the 'rope' ceiling moulding was picked out with a graining colour, as was also done in the Saloon and Dining Parlour.

WOODWORK

The woodwork is of the highest quality and, despite the changes made to the room, has been altered very little. It consists of four rows of linenfold panelling entirely covering the walls from floor to ceiling, unlike in the larger rooms of most domestic and civic buildings at this period, which were invariably panelled only up to the window sills. The vertical framing battens are quite simple and flat, while the horizontals have complex mouldings, with neat mitring at the junctions, giving the impression of a continuous series of 'picture frames' to each of the panels. The panels themselves are of different sizes, but are all equally thinly cut to about half an inch and are now in a very fragile condition.

At the top and bottom of each panel are carved coats of arms and insignia, which celebrate Sandys's high social status and position under the King. Sandys himself is represented by his coat of arms, ragged cross, initials 'WS', crest (the winged half-goat), and his badge of a rose merging with a sun (which would have been worn by his servants and attached to his personal possessions). Other people are identified by their 'rebus' (a sort of pun on their name), or their family war cry, like 'Coeur pour coeur' for Thomas Manners, Earl of Rutland, the brother of Sandys's daughter-in-law. The King and Queen are celebrated with the greatest number of motifs, Catherine of Aragon by the tower for Castile, the pomegranate for Aragon, and by the arms of the two Spanish kingdoms united in one shield. Other individuals or families represented are: the Bishops Fox of Winchester, Warham of Canterbury and Tunstall of London; the local families of Brocas (of Beaurepaire), Sir William Paulet (of Basing); and relations of Lord Sandys, such as Sir Walter Hungerford, Sir Humphrey Foster (sons-in-law) and Sir Reginald Bray (father-in-law). The delicacy of the carving suggests that it was originally left unpainted, which was usual for the period. It is transitional in style between the traditions of English Gothic carving and the new classical fashions imported from the Continent. The carving of the royal arms supported by cherubs over the east door is of a sophistication suggesting that it may have been commissioned specially from wood-carvers at the royal court. Elsewhere, classical motifs appear more crudely, in roundels, profile heads and the full-cheeked faces of zephyrs.

PICTURES

WALL FACING WINDOWS, LEFT TO RIGHT:

Manner of DANIEL MYTENS (c.1590–before 1648)
Called *Francis Bacon* (1561–1626)
Lord Chancellor under James I, scientist and philosopher.

ENGLISH, c.1625
Portrait of a Gentleman, called 'Duke of Buckingham'

ENGLISH, c.1615
Portrait of a Lady, called 'Countess of Essex'
The old identification is almost certainly wrong.

ENGLISH, c.1615
Portrait of a Gentleman, called 'Earl of Essex'
Pendant of 'Countess of Essex', it somewhat resembles portraits of Elizabeth I's favourite, Robert Devereux, 2nd Earl of Essex (1566–1601), but was painted after his execution.

LEFT OF DOOR TO THE TAPESTRY ROOM:

ENGLISH, c.1620
'Mrs Penobscot'
So identified in eighteenth-century inventories, but otherwise unknown.

RIGHT OF DOOR TO THE TAPESTRY ROOM:

ENGLISH, c.1623/4 (?)
Lady Frances Howard, Duchess of Richmond and Lennox (1578–1639)

FURNITURE

CHIMNEYPIECE WALL, NEAR END:

The oak table is English, c.1670, and is described by Wiggett as a table which was in use in the kitchen, to which he added the marble hearthstone from the Oak Gallery chimneypiece.

The painted and gilded pedestals are English, c.1750.

CHIMNEYPIECE WALL, FAR END:

The giltwood and black painted pier-table is English, c.1730, in the manner of William Kent (1685–1748) with an Italian scagliola slab top bearing the arms and motto ('To do what we feel') of Horace Walpole's father, Sir Robert Walpole, Prime Minister (1721–1742). It resembles side-tables at Houghton Hall, Norfolk, designed by William Kent for Sir Robert. Scagliola is made of pulverised selenite (a type of gypsum), which is painted, heated and polished to resemble inlaid marble.

CHIMNEYPIECE WALL, CENTRE:

The pair of walnut chairs with inlaid splats and cane seats and backs is English, c.1700.

CENTRE:

The eight mahogany leather-covered stools cost £3 12s each in 1753 and were invoiced by Vile and Cobb as

The scagliola table-top in the Oak Gallery bears the coat of arms of Sir Robert Walpole, Prime Minister and father of John Chute's friend, Horace Walpole

'8 large mahogany stools with carv'd feet and carv'd braceletts, stuff'd and cover'd with leather welted quilted and finished with burnish'd nails'. They were supplied to Anthony Chute for the Oak Gallery, where they were listed in 1754, and several retain their original eighteenth-century leather. The eighth stool was purchased by the National Trust, having been missing from The Vyne since 1776.

WINDOW WALL, SOUTH END:

The giltwood table with a marble top is English, *c.*1760, and is one of a pair displayed in the room by 1776. Their design relates to two drawings for tables, dated 1739, published in Batty and Thomas Langley's *The City and Country Builders' and Workmans' Treasury of Designs* (1756). A copy of this book is in the Library and was used by John Chute as a source for designs at The Vyne.

The tortoiseshell and ebony cabinet on a carved ebonised stand is Neapolitan, *c.*1650–70. The style of the painted decoration is similar to that of Luca Giordano (1632–1705). It was probably purchased in Italy by John Chute.

The eighteenth-century stained glass roundel by John Price has recently been returned to the bay window.

SCULPTURE AND BRONZES

The great majority of the sculpture and bronzes was purchased by Wiggett Chute in 1845–7. The pair of Italian mid-eighteenth-century busts of Roman emperors is part of a set of four; the other pair is on the principal staircase.

ON TABLE LEFT OF CHIMNEYPIECE:

The pair of reliefs of a satyr and bacchante is Flemish, late seventeenth- or early eighteenth-century, purchased by Wiggett for £9.

FAR END OF CHIMNEYPIECE WALL:

The three bronze busts of Henry VIII, Charles I and Oliver Cromwell are English, *c.*1840–5, and were bought by Wiggett. He paid £13 3s 6d for the bust of Charles I, which is after Hubert le Sueur. The other smaller bronzes were also bought by Wiggett.

THE GALLERY BEDROOM AND SOUTH BEDROOM

The space now occupied by these rooms may originally have formed the King's lodgings, where Henry VIII would have slept during his visits in 1531 and 1535. In the 1754 and 1776 inventories, the Gallery Bedroom and South Bedroom are described as the Yellow Chamber and South Damask Bedchamber respectively. They became the White Bedroom and Dressing Room by 1842, furnished with white-ground chintz bed-hangings and curtains, and chintz-patterned Brussels carpet.

The present arrangement of the rooms allows for part of the collection, previously in store, to be displayed in a domestic setting.

PICTURES

In the Gallery Bedroom is displayed a selection from a collection of 43 watercolours on vellum card and paper generously given to the National Trust by Miss Hodsall. They were painted by Elizabeth (d. 1842), wife of William John Chute, and her sister, Augusta, and their governess, Margaret Meen, between 1784 and 1807. Some were executed at The Vyne, and others at Suttons (Stapleford Tawney), Essex, the estate of Charles Smith, who married Augusta in 1798. The South Bedroom displays family portraits, pastels and watercolours, including the donors, Sir Charles and Lady Chute.

FURNITURE

The two linen presses contain a collection of dress and accoutrements dating from the middle of the eighteenth to the middle of the nineteenth century. (Not always open to view.)

The mahogany bedstead in the Gallery Bedroom is English, early nineteenth-century of country manufacture.

The serpentine-fronted mahogany dressing table in the Gallery Bedroom is English, *c.*1760, the top drawer fitted to receive *toilette* articles, English, *c.*1760.

The mahogany tester bedstead in the South Bedroom is English, *c.*1845. The hangings are a recent acquisition, the printed cotton dates from the early twentieth century.

Visitors descend to the ground floor from the South Bedroom via the south landing of the Staircase Hall.

THE PRINT ROOM

In 1754 this was described as the 'Little Dining Parlour', and the plaster ceiling and cornice probably belong to this period. The panelling between the windows is reused and altered earlier wooden decoration. John Chute renamed this room the 'Strawberry Parlour' in honour of the 'Committee of Taste' which met at The Vyne and Strawberry Hill. It is possible Walpole used this and the neighbouring room when he was John's guest here.

Caroline Workman describes the changes made to the decoration of the room in 1804: 'The prints were put up in the little parlour, and as my brothers happened to be at The Vyne, they greatly assisted in doing so, particularly James who showed so much taste in those matters. The prints had always been kept in a large portfolio in the gallery on large black stools.' Wiggett Chute remarked in his *Reminiscences* that some of the engravings were too valuable for 'such a situation'. By 1959 they had deteriorated beyond repair, and were mostly replaced with the group now displayed, which came from the Liechtenstein collection; the walls were repainted at the same time. The majority are engravings after seventeenth- and eighteenth-century Italian and French Old Masters, including Correggio, Poussin, Raphael, Le Brun and Agostino Carracci. A detailed handlist is available. The fashion for print rooms grew from the middle of the eighteenth century until the early nineteenth century.

FURNITURE

The country-made elm desk, English, *c.*1725–50, copies an earlier and finer London equivalent *c.*1710.

The Market Stall; after Frans Snyders. One of the Old Master engravings pasted to the walls of the Print Room

THE STRAWBERRY PARLOUR

This possibly formed one of the 'Base Chambers' described in the 1541 inventory. To the right of the window a Tudor doorway is concealed behind the panelling, which has no doubt been reorganised. The door joinery and ceiling are eighteenth-century (possibly the work of Anthony Chute), and by 1754 the room was called the Green Canopy Bedchamber (recent paint analysis of the room found traces of varnished green paint, which was removed by Chaloner William Chute at the end of the nineteenth century). By 1776 John Chute had removed the bed, and the room became the Green Parlour. Wiggett Chute described it in 1872 as his study and 'which I call my own, but which appears to be the general place of deposit for articles having no other home'. Later it was called the Strawberry Parlour (the name once given the Print Room).

PICTURES

The room is mainly hung with architectural drawings by John Chute and prints associated with Strawberry Hill and its circle.

? FRENCH or SWISS, eighteenth-century
A Girl with a Tambourine

ENGLISH, *c*.1750
Thomas Lobb Chute (1721–90)
He inherited The Vyne on the death of his cousin, John Chute, in 1776, when he changed his name to Chute.

OVER FIREPLACE:

ENGLISH, eighteenth-century
A Seascape

FURNITURE

The walnut writing-cabinet is English, *c*.1690.

The two pairs of back stools are English, mahogany, 1750–3, and are part of a larger set of seat furniture supplied by Vile and Cobb (including four arm-chairs now no longer at The Vyne), possibly identi-fiable with an invoice dated 30 March 1753. The linen loose case covers with appliqué embroidered 'slips' in the mid eighteenth-century style, were probably made by Laura, Lady Chute, during the early twentieth century.

The spinet, English, *c*.1740, is a recent gift to The Vyne and recalls the spinet listed here in 1776.

The longcase clock is by Thomas Tompion (1639–1713), the most famous English clockmaker of his age.

THE STONE GALLERY

This occupies the whole ground floor of the west wing, and may have been a single space since Tudor times. (Recent archaeological work has revealed a doorway leading to the demolished tower at the south-west corner and larger Tudor windows, now partially blocked up, on the east and west walls.)

In 1753 Anthony Chute commissioned William Blake of Basingstoke to lay the present 'Portland Stone pavement with Black marble dotts', with a black marble border to the sides. Chute may also have put up the Tudor Revival ceiling, which is similar to that in the Oak Gallery directly above. By 1754 the room was called 'The Greenhouse', and in 1780 Mrs Lybbe Powys described: 'Two long galleries . . . the other they make a greenhouse of in winter, and they say it has a most pleasing effect to

Terracotta medallion of the Roman Emperor Probus (d. AD282), who introduced vines to Britain. Probably made in the workshop of Giovanni da Maiano in the 1520s, it is one of the earliest examples of Italian Renaissance sculpture in this country

The Stone Gallery in 1877; watercolour by Elizabeth Chute

walk thro', the oranges, myrtles etc. ranged on each side.' According to Caroline Workman (née Wiggett), who lived at The Vyne early in the nineteenth century (see p. 61), the orange trees were moved out to the terrace on the south front every summer, with geraniums (in pots) inside the balustrade, which looked 'very cheerful'.

Wiggett Chute, who moved to The Vyne in 1842, repaired the floor and installed the heating system around the walls, but gave up keeping plants in the room which became something of a day nursery, and later a theatre, for his children. His daughter Elizabeth's watercolour of 1877 (on display in the West Corridor) shows the room at this time. The series of watercolours by Elizabeth and her mother, Martha, on display in the house gives a fascinating insight into Victorian life at The Vyne.

FURNITURE

The oak plant tables around the perimeter of the room installed by Wiggett Chute *c.*1845 incorporate as supports the balusters of a seventeenth-century staircase.

SCULPTURE

EAST WALL, OVER CHIMNEYPIECE:

The terracotta medallion bust is of the Roman Emperor Probus (d. AD 282), who authorised the introduction of vines into Britain. It resembles similar medallions made by the Florentine Giovanni da Maiano for Hampton Court in 1521, which are among the earliest examples of the Italian Renaissance in Britain. When it arrived at The Vyne is unclear, as the 1754 inventory lists only one large picture for the room, which was probably hung over the chimneypiece. John Chute may have obtained the roundel after the Tudor 'Holbein' gate in Whitehall was demolished in 1759–60.

BUSTS

John Chute wrote to his brother Anthony in 1753, listing a set of eleven plaster busts 'as good as any we could have got by sending for them on purpose from Italy', which he had seen in London and which he was anxious to acquire for the Oak Gallery. The three plaster busts on display in the Stone Gallery are the survivors of that set. Some of the Antique busts and fragments once formed part of the Lyde collection, formerly at Stoke Park, Wiltshire, the home of Elizabeth Smith, William John Chute's wife.

The tablets with Greek and Latin inscriptions were a present from Horace Walpole to John Chute. Wiggett Chute moved them here from the Chapel, and added the frames.

The fragmentary figure of Eros asleep, under the 'Elizabethan Table' is a Roman copy or an adaptation of a Hellenistic statue of the second or first century BC. It was a popular subject in late Hellenistic and Roman art.

THE FURTHER DRAWING ROOM

This is the first of a suite of rooms along the north front of the house. It was probably built in the seventeenth century, but of that period not a trace remains visible. The precise date of the extensive eighteenth-century alterations to the joinery and ceilings is unclear. Anthony Chute may have played a part, possibly by introducing the wainscot and doors. The rococo papier-mâché ceiling decorations installed here and in the Ante-Room and Large Drawing Room beyond are traditionally assumed to be John Chute's work, and certainly the cornice has always been decorated in black and gold, which was a favourite combination for 'Strawberry Hill' taste. This suggests that John remodelled the ceiling and cornice, perhaps in the 1760s.

TEXTILES

The *silk and linen brocatelle wall-hangings*, Italian *c*.1730. The silk, as well as the stamped and gilded parchment fillet covering the nailed edge, is a now rare survival of a fashionable eighteenth-century

The Further Drawing Room was used as a class-room between 1919 and 1932

decorative scheme. However, the hangings in this room and the Ante-Room are not listed in the 1776 inventory, and may, therefore, have been brought to The Vyne by John's heir, Thomas Lobb Chute, from his Charles Street town house after that date (it was quite usual to reuse wall-hangings in the eighteenth century). The choice may have been influenced by Walpole, who wrote in 1760: 'I don't approve of damask at all, for as there will be no pictures in the chamber, nothing is more triste than a single colour.' Brocatelle has a silk weft and a silk and linen warp, which produces, when new, a greater contrast of pattern and ground colour than damask. There may also have been an element of antiquarianism in John's decision to use brocatelle of a design that was rather old-fashioned by 1768.

Wiggett Chute installed the chimneypiece. The room has recently been redecorated to suggest how it may have appeared when the brocatelle was installed, albeit taking account of its faded and much repaired condition.

The worsted pile carpet is English, c.1815 and was restored c.1960. Once vivid in colour, it is a fragment of a much larger carpet.

PICTURES

LEFT OF STONE GALLERY DOOR:

ROSALBA GIOVANNA CARRIERA (1675–1757/8)
John Chute
Ink on paper, 1741

OVER FIREPLACE:

VINCENTE GINER (active c.1680)
Fantastic Architecture with Figures
Bought by Wiggett Chute in 1843.

RIGHT OF FIREPLACE, TOP:

JOHANN HEINRICH MÜNTZ (1727–98) after
POMPEO BATONI (1708–87)
John Chute (1701–76), 1756
He created the Tomb Chamber and Staircase Hall in memory of his famous ancestor, Speaker Chute. This copy was painted for his friend Horace Walpole, who employed this Swiss artist to decorate Strawberry Hill. Bought by Wiggett at the 1842 Strawberry Hill sale.

BELOW:

JOHANN HEINRICH MÜNTZ (1727–98)
The Vyne from the North-West, 1755

An idealised view, showing a tower at the south-west (far right) corner and a second summer-house, which were never built. Also painted for Walpole.

LEFT OF WINDOW, TOP:

ROSALBA CARRIERA (1675–1758)
Francis Whithead (1719–51)
Pastel
Probably painted in Venice in 1741, when he was on the Grand Tour with his cousin, John Chute.

BELOW:

JOHN CHUTE (1701–76) and JOHN HOBCROFT (active 1743–79)
Two Architectural Designs for Donnington Grove
The Berkshire home of the antiquary James Andrews was designed by Chute in 1763–5.

RIGHT OF WINDOW, TOP:

Attributed to ARTHUR POND (1701–58)
? Margaret Nichol, later Marchioness of Carnarvon (d. 1768)
Pastel
A cousin of the Chutes, she was at one time engaged to Francis Whithead (see p. 53)

BELOW:

JOHN CHUTE (1701–76) and JOHN HOBCROFT (active 1743–79)
Two Architectural Designs for Donnington Grove

NORTH WALL, RIGHT:

A mahogany case containing nine family miniatures, including Batoni's portrait of John Chute, dated 1746 (see folder for descriptions).

LEFT OF DOOR TO CHINA ROOM, TOP:

JEAN-BAPTISTE OUDRY (1686–1755)
A Pointer and a Pheasant in a Landscape, 1724

RIGHT OF DOOR TO CHINA ROOM, TOP:

JEAN-BAPTISTE OUDRY (1686–1755)
A Fox putting up a Brace of Partridges, 1724
Oudry was one of the greatest French painters of animals.

BELOW:

JOHANN HEINRICH MÜNTZ (1727–98) after
GASPARD POUSSIN (1615–75)
A Classical Landscape

*A Pointer and a
Pheasant in a
Landscape; by Jean-
Baptiste Oudry, 1724
(Further Drawing
Room)*

BELOW:

JOHANN HEINRICH MÜNTZ (1727–98) after PAUL
BRIL (1554–1626)
A Rocky Landscape with a Hermit

FURNITURE

WEST WALL, LEFT:

Lacquer cabinet with giltwood stand, English, *c*.1695.
The exterior and interior of the cabinet are decorated with groups of figures, a flowering tree and
pagoda-roofed buildings. This cabinet and another
at the V&A are the only documented examples that
directly copy the designs published by John Stalker
and George Parker in *Treatise of Japanning and
Varnishing* (1688). In 1776 these two cabinets stood
in the Library.

WEST WALL, RIGHT:

Lacquer cabinet with giltwood stand, English, *c*.1685.
The lacquer of the cabinet was repaired in London
during the late seventeenth century when the
brown borders were added. The lacquer facings of
the individual interior drawers do not relate to each

other stylistically. It could be that the panels of
lacquer were reused from a larger, damaged object
such as a screen that was applied to a London-made
carcass imitating this traditional Asian form of
cabinet.

FAR WALL:

*The giltwood and black-painted agate-topped pier-table
and pier-glass* above are English, *c*.1760.

CENTRE OF ROOM:

The mahogany gate-leg tea-table is English, *c*.1753. It is
probably the 'mahogany table with 8 legs', for
which William Vile and John Cobb charged £1 10s
on 30 March 1753.

The seat furniture was made by William France and
John Bradburne, *c*.1765, and supplied to John Chute.
They are part of a set of five settees, six open
armchairs and eight single chairs, described in more
detail in the Large Drawing Room (p. 24).

RIGHT-HAND WALL:

The pair of mahogany tables, *c*.1765, was supplied by
France and Bradburne for £11.

CERAMICS

ON CHIMNEYPIECE:

The garniture of Sèvres porcelain has been assembled recently with the help of the Victoria & Albert Museum. On 14 November 1765 the Rev. William Cole, who had accompanied Horace Walpole on a trip to Paris, recorded in his diary: 'We went to the shop of Madame Dulac.... Mr. Walpole, among other things, bought 3 most beautiful vases for a chimney, of blew Enamel, set in gilt Copper, for Mr. Chute of the Vine in Hampshire; they cost 19 guineas, and were the most elegant Ornaments for the Place they were designed, the middle one being larger than the 2 others.' The vases are of soft paste Sèvres porcelain imitating Chinese monochrome wares and are decorated with the dark blue glaze known as *bleu nouveau*. The earliest documented example of the central potpourri vase or *vase cloche* was supplied to Madame de Pompadour in late 1763 or early 1764 and is now thought to be the vase at the Wadsworth Atheneum, Hartford, Connecticut. The lid is a recent restoration, generously paid for by Sèvres and Trust supporters.

ON THE CABINETS ON THE WEST WALL:

The two black basalt oil lamps are Wedgwood, *c.*1785. The body is a variant of a vase form known as the Michelangelo lamp, but is in fact of Hellenistic origin. The figures on the right-hand lamp are adapted from a silver-gilt crucifix by Antonio Gentile da Faenza (1519–1609).

THE CHINA ROOM

This room was decorated in the eighteenth century at the same time as its larger neighbours. By 1888 it was called the China Room.

PICTURES

ELIZABETH CHUTE (d. 1913)
*The Large Drawing Room, c.*1860
Watercolour

FURNITURE

The casket of ebony with panels of pietra dura mounted in ormolu and encrusted with semi-precious stones is Italian, *c.*1720; the giltwood rococo stand is English, possibly 1752, and unites a Grand Tour souvenir with English craftsmanship. The casket was made in the Grand Ducal Workshops in Florence, in the *Opificio delle Pietre Dure*, designed by its last great director, Giovanni Battista Foggini (1652–1725), as there are several drawings by his hand relating to the casket.

The mahogany side-chairs are English, *c.*1765, from the set of seat furniture by France and Bradburne.

CERAMICS

The sixteen opaque glass plates, coffee beakers and associated dishes known as 'lattimo' or 'Murano' ware, are Venetian, *c.*1740, and are rare souvenirs of the Grand Tour. When Horace Walpole, John Chute and the Earl of Lincoln were in Venice in June–July 1741, they visited the glassworks on Murano, and

The pietra dura casket was bought by John Chute in 1741–5 while in Florence on his Grand Tour. He added the rococo stand and glass cover

*A mid-seventeenth-century English tin-glazed earthenware
dish in the style of the sixteenth-century French potter,
Bernard Palissy (China Room)*

each ordered two dozen plates of Venetian glass.
These were available only by special order and
were supplied with the help of the British Consul,
Joseph Smith. They depict views of Venice, generally after etchings by Marieschi (1703) and engravings by Visentini after Canaletto (1735).

The four dishes and five plates are from Castelli in
southern Italy, *c.*1730, one of the leading makers of
eighteenth-century Italian maiolica.

Other ceramics displayed include *Chinese blue-and-
white porcelain* of the first half of the eighteenth
century and English mid-eighteenth-century delft.

The pair of moulded tin-glazed dishes is English, probably made in Southwark, *c.*1650–70. They are
derived from the famous dishes produced by
Bernard Palissy during the sixteenth century in
France, of which this 'la Fécondité' design with
variations for the border decoration, was the most
popular.

The pair of porcelain plates is Chinese, Kangxi, *c.*1700.

THE LARGE DRAWING
ROOM

The room was referred to in the 1754 inventory as
the 'Best Parlour' and by Walpole in his 'Inventionary' as the 'Great Parlour'. The ceiling has

recently been repainted and the pictures and furniture rearranged to restore more of the room's eighteenth-century character. By 1776 it contained five
paintings (Walpole had wanted to add portraits of
Francis Whithead, Thomas Gray, Richard Bentley
and himself as overdoors to reinforce the theme of
the friendship of the Strawberry Committee).
According to Caroline Workman, in the early nineteenth century the room was used only on dinner
party days (ie infrequently) and the furniture was
still arranged around the walls in the formal, eighteenth-century fashion, when not in use.

The brocatelle wall-hangings, which are described
in the 1776 inventory, were repaired by Wiggett
Chute a hundred years later using parts of the
festoon curtains, which were of the same material.
Lady Meade-Fetherstonhaugh repaired them again
in 1960–1 for the National Trust.

CHIMNEYPIECE

John Chute ordered a marble chimneypiece from
Thomas Carter for £70 for this room, but after his
death in 1776, his heir, Thomas Lobb Chute,
refused to accept it. The present chimneypiece is in
fact made of three separate parts, and was assembled
by Wiggett Chute in the mid-nineteenth century.
The caryatids were united with a large carved
frame (probably made to John Webb's design),
which was once an overmantel for the chimneypiece now in the Library. (Elizabeth Chute recorded
the original arrangement in a watercolour.) Its
painted and gilded decoration, first applied when it
was assembled for this room, has recently been
revealed.

PICTURES

EAST (NEAR) WALL:

GABRIEL MATHIAS (1719–1804)
John Chute (1701–76), 1758
He holds one of his drawings for remodelling The
Vyne in the Gothick style, which was not carried
out. In the background is the portico on the garden
front.

FIREPLACE WALL, LEFT:

After Sir ANTHONY VAN DYCK (1599–1641)
Called *Dorothy North, Lady Dacre (Mrs Chute)*
(1605–98)
Traditionally said to be of Speaker Chute's second
wife.

The Large Drawing Room

FURNITURE

OVER FIREPLACE:

DUTCH, ? seventeenth-century
A Wooded Landscape with an Avenue

RIGHT OF FIREPLACE:

Manner of Sir ANTHONY VAN DYCK (1599–1641)
Ann Skory, Mrs Chaloner Chute
She married Speaker Chute in 1627 as his first wife.
Perhaps an eighteenth-century pastiche.

WEST (FAR) WALL:

ALEXIS-SIMON BELLE (1674–1734)
Portrait of a Nun, known as Winifred Cufaude, 1703
Said to be of the daughter of Symeon Cufaude,
whose family lived next to The Vyne. She wears
the habit of an Augustinian Canoness.

WINDOW WALL:

The pair of carved giltwood pier-glasses is English,
*c.*1730, and incorporates the Chute crest between
their broken pediments. The pair of mahogany card
tables is English, *c.*1760, and is probably that listed
here in 1776.

REMAINDER OF ROOM:

*The set of two settees and six armchairs, c.*1765, is part of
the group of furniture already seen in the Further
Drawing Room and China Room. By 1759 William
France (1734–73) was in the employment of Vile
and Cobb, suppliers of furniture to The Vyne; it
was probably not long after he went into partner-
ship with John Bradburne (1750–81), in May–June
1764, that they were recommended to supply furniture to John Chute.

The Large Drawing Room in 1860; watercolour by Elizabeth Chute

Although some of the furniture now at The Vyne was originally made for the family's London house, the two large settees and accompanying armchairs undoubtedly were commissioned specifically for the Large Drawing Room, to which they have been returned recently. During 2000–01 this furniture was improved by restoring the earlier shape of the upholstery and recovering it with a damask based on the brocatelle hangings of the Large Drawing Room.

CERAMICS

The pair of baluster form jars, Chinese *famille verte*, early nineteenth century, were supplied to Wiggett Chute by the dealer Edward Holmes Baldock.

THE VESTIBULE

The Vestibule at the north end of the staircase was designed by John Chute in the early 1770s. Its Neo-classical character represents a marked change in architectural taste when compared with his rococo decoration of the rooms just visited. It is likely that a staircase occupied at least part of this space in the sixteenth and seventeenth centuries.

FURNITURE

The 'Roman Altar' at the centre of the room, designed by John Chute for this position, is English, *c.*1770. The altar is predominantly veneered with padouk, a tropical hardwood imported from South-east Asia and rarely used in English furniture of this period. The padouk veneer, when new, was purple-red in hue. Its present reddish-brown colour is due to exposure to light.

John Chute's placing of the altar in the Vestibule was a conscious emulation of the Antique Roman practice of placing an altar to the household gods in the vestibule of houses.

Two hall-chairs (see page 9).

SCULPTURE

The pair of bronzed plaster figures, *c.*1810, of a Vestal Virgin and Sibyl, is English. They derive from prototypes manufactured in artificial 'Coade stone' by Mrs Eleanor Coade and first appear in etchings of the 1770s–80s.

THE SALOON

The stone chimneypiece was probably carved by Edward Marshall for Chaloner Chute in the late 1650s. By 1754 'the Great Hall', as it was described, was painted white, and the cornice may also have

The Saloon

been introduced by this date. John Chute evidently repainted the panelling and cornice dark blue, and partly gilded the cornice. Gilt bosses (probably of lead) were added to the centres of the panels and rails. After 1776 the room was used occasionally for dining; by the mid-nineteenth century, when Wiggett Chute and his family were living at The Vyne, it had become a drawing-room. Wiggett Chute raised the centre of the ceiling and added the diagonal mouldings, graining the room to imitate light oak, and gilding parts of the cornice. The room was later grained to a darker colour before it was stripped of all its paint in the early twentieth century by Sir Charles Chute, who also removed the gilt bosses.

The room has recently been rearranged to reflect the Wiggett period. In an attempt to reunite the colours of the different decorative elements, dark graining has been restored to doors, architraves and cornices, and gilt bosses reintroduced.

PICTURES

Wiggett Chute's crowded hang has been reassembled.

WINDOW WALL, FAR LEFT:

MARTHA CHUTE (d. 1888)
The Saloon, 1857
Drawing

MARTHA CHUTE (d. 1888)
The Saloon, 1860
Watercolour

WINDOW WALL, FAR RIGHT:

After CORREGIO (1494–1534)
The Head of a Child

BERKHEYDEN
A farmyard scene

The Saloon in 1860; watercolour by Martha Chute

EAST (FAR) WALL, OVER DOOR:

MARTHA CHUTE (d. 1888) after AELBERT CUYP
(1620–91)
A River Scene
This copy after the great Dutch landscapist was
hanging here by the 1880s.

RIGHT OF DOOR, CLOCKWISE FROM LEFT:

FREDERICK RICHARD SAY (1827–60)
William Lyde Wiggett Chute (1800–79), 1843
He took the name Chute on inheriting The Vyne
from his cousin Thomas in 1827. He modernised
the house and estate after a period of neglect.

After NICOLAS POUSSIN (1594–1665)
The Sabines in the Temple

JOHANN HEINRICH MÜNTZ (1727–98)
View of The Vyne from the North East

FREDERICK RICHARD SAY (1827–60)
*Martha Chute (d. 1888) and her son, Chaloner (1838–
92), 1843*
Painted six years after her marriage to Wiggett
Chute. Chaloner wrote the history of The Vyne.

LEFT OF FIREPLACE, OVER DOOR:

ENGLISH, *c.*1615
? *Dudley, 3rd Baron North (1581–1666)*
The father of Speaker Chute's second wife. Musi-
cian, writer and discoverer of the springs at
Tunbridge Wells in 1606.

LEFT OF FIREPLACE, CLOCKWISE FROM TOP LEFT:

JOHANN HEINRICH MÜNTZ (1727–98)
A River Scene with Rock Banks and a Waterfall
Probably in the Dining Parlour in John Chute's
time, serving as an overdoor.

Manner of PAOLO VERONESE (1528–88)
The Finding of Moses
Bought by Wiggett Chute in 1847.

Manner of SALVATOR ROSA (1615–73)
Architecture and Figures or *The Sentinel in the
Graveyard*

Manner of JACOB DE WET (active 1633–75)
Paul and Barnabas at Lystra

OVER FIREPLACE:

? JOHANN HEINRICH MÜNTZ (1727–98)
An Italian Landscape
A fantasy view with the Colosseum on the left.
Moved here by Wiggett Chute from the old Tapes-

try Room, where it had been in a frame which he converted into the overmantel of the present Large Drawing Room fireplace.

RIGHT OF FIREPLACE, CLOCKWISE FROM TOP LEFT:

After GABRIEL METSU (1629–67)
The Music Party

MARTHA CHUTE (d. 1888)
A Classical Landscape
In the style of the French painter Claude (1600–82).

ELIZABETH CHUTE (1843–1913) in the manner of PHILIPS WOUWERMANS (1619–68)
A Roadside Halt

After PAOLO VERONESE (1528–88)
The Holy Family, with the infant St John and SS Justina, Francis and Jerome
The original is in the Accademia, Venice.

OVER DOOR:

ENGLISH, *c.*1595
Sir John North (?1551–97)
Grandfather of Speaker Chute's second wife.

WEST (NEAR) WALL, LEFT TO RIGHT:

UNKNOWN
Mary Chute, sister of John Chute, mid-eighteenth century

Attributed to SICIOLANTE DA SERMONETA (1521–*c.*1580)
The Holy Family with the infant SS John and Elizabeth
A Mannerist painting in the tradition of Raphael. Probably bought by Wiggett Chute in 1847.

UNKNOWN
Anne Chute, sister of John Chute, mid-eighteenth century
Anne accompanied John on one of his Grand Tours.

OVER DOOR:

FRANCESCO ZUCCARELLI (1702–88)
Landscape with Rocks

FURNITURE

WINDOW WALL:

The three carved and giltwood pier-glasses are English, *c.*1745.

The pair of rosewood and brass inlaid card-tables is English, *c.*1825–30.

The set of four bronze lamps is English, *c.*1830–5. The lamp is in the form of an antique rhyton (drinking cup) with a dolphin's-head spout. The design is taken from a burial monument on the Appian Way in Rome, published in Piranesi's *Vasi, Candelabri, Cippi, Sarcofagi . . .* (1778).

CENTRE OF ROOM AND ON FAR WALL:

*The remainder of the France and Bradburne set of seat furniture, c.*1765.

The circular 'centre' table, the tilt-top 'breakfast' table and the pair of card tables, all *en suite*, are veneered with rosewood and inlaid with brass, and are English *c.*1830. Purchased by Wiggett Chute at the Marquess of Winchester's sale in 1844.

CHIMNEYPIECE WALL:

The pair of serpentine and ormolu-mounted commodes in the French rococo style is English, *c.*1760–5, probably by the leading French *émigré* cabinetmaker of the 1760s and 1770s, Pierre Langlois. They were probably supplied for John Chute's town house and brought to The Vyne by Thomas Lobb Chute; they can be seen in Martha Chute's watercolour of this room (illustrated opposite).

The japanned work-table is English, *c.*1830.

NEAR WALL:

The harewood and kingwood bureau plat, or writing-table, with ormolu mounts is in the French style of 1730–40. It was probably among the furniture and ornaments bought by Wiggett Chute in May 1843 for £136 2s from Edward Holmes Baldock (*c.*1777–1843), a leading furniture dealer and restorer, whose clients included George IV. He also supplied porcelain for The Vyne.

The table clock in the Louis XV style, *c.*1750, is French, and was also supplied by Baldock in 1843.

MUSICAL INSTRUMENTS

The piano of veneered rosewood is English, *c.*1846, and is a good example of Broadwood's Patent Repetitive Grand (Broadwood's 1838 modification of the double escapement action invented by Sébastian Erard and patented in England in 1821). When Chopin visited London in 1848, he used two similar instruments.

The Dining Parlour

The Grecian harp is an Erard (no.4006), *c.*1825–27, with a mechanism first patented in 1811, and was a gift to the National Trust.

THE DINING PARLOUR

Two rooms originally occupied this space, and the Tudor panelling must therefore have been reorganised after the present room was created. It is described as the Dining Parlour in 1754 and 1776, and was painted by John Chute in a pale blue. Wiggett Chute furnished it as a dining-room, purchasing fourteen dining-chairs in 1843 (sold in 1956) and a dining-table from the Marquess of Winchester's sale in 1844. Martha Chute's water-colour of *c.*1860 (illustrated on p. 30) depicts the room with the table laid for breakfast. Wiggett grained the panelling to imitate light oak, as he had done in the Saloon, and substituted the back of a sideboard for the chimneypiece he removed to the present Tapestry Room. Eight of the linenfold panels had been lost sometime before 1956. During conservation work in 1998 these panels were recarved, completing the scheme of panelling, and graining was reintroduced on the doors and cornice, with the same rationale as in the Saloon. The Trust hopes to replace the missing window curtains as funding becomes available.

PICTURES

The crowded picture-hang created by Wiggett Chute has recently been revived, where possible.

IN DOORWAY:

MARTHA CHUTE (d. 1888)
The Dining Parlour, c.1860
Watercolour
This view has been used as a guide in rehanging the pictures.

FACING WALL, LEFT OF DOOR, TOP:

ENGLISH, 1615
Henry Barker, aged 79
Speaker Chute's daughter, Anne, married into the Barker family of Chiswick. This may be an ancestor.

BELOW:

ENGLISH, 1579
Chrysogona Baker, Lady Dacre, aged six (d. 1616)
The daughter of Sir Richard Baker of Sissinghurst, she married Henry, 12th Lord Dacre in 1589.

OVER DOOR:

JOHANN HEINRICH MÜNTZ (1727–98)
A Landscape with River Scene

RIGHT OF DOOR:

ENGLISH, c.1720
Edward Chute (1658–1722)
The father of John Chute.

Attributed to AGOSTINO MASUCCI (1692–1768)
The Holy Family

ENGLISH, c.1700
Elizabeth Chute, Mrs Thomas Lobb (d. 1725)
The daughter of Thomas Chute of Pickenham, Norfolk. Her son Thomas inherited The Vyne in 1776.

LEFT OF FIREPLACE:

SEBASTIAN PETHER (c.1790–1844)
Moonlight, 1841
Pether painted landscapes of this kind in the style of his more famous father, Abraham 'Moonlight' Pether. Bought by Wiggett Chute in 1843.

OVER FIREPLACE:

After GUIDO RENI (1585–1642)
Aurora
A nineteenth-century copy of Reni's ceiling fresco of the goddess of the dawn in the Casino Rospigliosi in Rome.

RIGHT OF FIREPLACE:

SEBASTIAN PETHER (c.1790–1844)
Sunrise, 1842
Pendant to *Moonlight*.

The Dining Parlour, c.1860; watercolour by Martha Chute

WALL, RIGHT OF FIREPLACE, CLOCKWISE FROM TOP LEFT:

ENGLISH, ? eighteenth-century
Chaloner Chute II (1630–66)
Son of Speaker Chute. Perhaps an eighteenth-century pastiche, modelled on Robert Walker's portrait of Oliver Cromwell's son, Richard.

Attributed to JOHN CLOSTERMAN (1660–1711/13)
? Chaloner Chute III (1656–85)
Grandson of Speaker Chute. But possibly of his younger brother, Thomas (*c*.1660–*c*.1705).

ENGLISH, *c*.1700
Thomas Lennard Chute
The son of Thomas Chute of Pickenham, he married his cousin, Catherine, daughter of Edward Chute of The Vyne.

After ? HANS HOLBEIN the Younger
(1497–1543)
Charles Brandon, 1st Duke of Suffolk (1485–1545)
Leading figure at the court of Henry VIII, whose sister he married, painted at the end of his life. The original in Munich was destroyed in the Second World War.

After HANS EWORTH (1520–?1574)
Mary Neville, Lady Dacre (d. ?1576)
The portrait included in the picture is of her husband, Thomas, 9th Lord Dacre, who had been executed for murder in 1541. The original, painted about 1555–8, is in the National Gallery of Canada, Ottawa.

NETHERLANDISH, *c*.1520–30
The Virgin and Child with St Anne

Manner of SASSOFERRATO (1609–*c*.1685)
The Virgin and Child
Bought by Wiggett Chute in 1847.

After HANS HOLBEIN the Younger (1497–1543)
Henry VIII (1491–1547)
William Sandys entertained the King at The Vyne in 1510, 1531 and 1535.

OVER DOOR:

JOHANN HEINRICH MÜNTZ (1727–98)
A Gothic Gateway by a River

RIGHT OF DOOR, TOP:

ENGLISH, *c*.1650
Catherine Lennard, Mrs Chaloner Chute
The daughter of Richard, 13th Baron Dacre, whose widow, Dorothy, subsequently married Speaker

Chute as his second wife. Catherine married Speaker Chute's son by his first wife.

BELOW:

ENGLISH, *c*.1620
? Charles Chute, MP
Father of Speaker Chute.

WOODWORK

Although brought from another part of the house, the Tudor linenfold panelling (resembling stiffly folded cloth) gives a good impression of how a fully panelled room would have appeared in the sixteenth century. William Harrison in his *Description of England* (1577) said that such rooms were 'not a little commended, made warm and much more close than otherwise they would be'. The small panels are fitted from floor to ceiling without any great sense of proportion to the room as a whole in a manner typical of smaller, private rooms in the early sixteenth century, such as the downstairs parlour rooms of Haddon Hall, Derbyshire, or Dorney Court, Berkshire, in that respect. By the late seventeenth century the panelling was painted white.

FURNITURE

WINDOW WALL:

The circular giltwood mirror is English, *c*.1750, and displays the sun god Apollo's mask in the centre, with a radiating sunburst. It is listed here in the 1754 inventory.

CENTRE AND BY WALLS:

The dining table of mahogany with ebonised banding is English, *c*.1820, based on a typical design dating from the second quarter of the eighteenth century.

The set of twelve walnut dining-chairs with baluster form backs, is English, *c*.1715. *The embroidered over-the-rail seat upholstery*, executed by Laura, Lady Chute and dating from the 1940s, is wrought in *gros* and *petit point* stitches. The design is copied from the Antwerp tiles in the Chapel.

The pair of side-tables with walnut frames and Tinos marble tops is English, *c*.1730.

The pair of mahogany urns on pedestals is English, *c*.1765–70, and possibly by France and Bradburne.

THE ANTE-CHAPEL

In the sixteenth century the Ante-Chapel would have formed part of the chapel itself, where the household would have witnessed the Mass. The alignment of a surviving door in the east corridor and a blocked doorway on the south wall suggest that the household would have entered the Chapel from outside the house.

Today, it represents the antiquarian Gothick taste of John Chute and his Strawberry Committee friends, who wanted to provide a suitably ancient-looking ante-room to the genuinely Tudor Chapel beyond. In 1755 Walpole suggested further Goth-icising the Ante-Chapel so that it should 'be finished as the end is', which implies that Chute extended the decoration already existing on the Chapel side of the room. The new panelling comprises merely thin strips of wood in a fret-like pattern, painted dark brown with touches of gold and blue. The geometric pattern of moulded wooden ribs, sug-gestive of fan vaulting, was probably pinned to the ceiling at the same time and serves no structural purpose.

The floor was originally paved with stone, which

The Ante-Chapel

was replaced with boards by Wiggett Chute in the mid-nineteenth century.

STAINED GLASS

Walpole proposed installing armorial glass and a painted Chute family tree. The present heraldic panes were mostly inserted in the twentieth century by Sir Charles Chute, and came from the Holy Trinity Chapel at Basingstoke. However, it is possible that some may originally have belonged to the more modest scheme once in the Chapel (see p. 36). Two similar panels of armorial stained glass, probably associated with this group, are in the windows of the Whistler Room at Mottisfont Abbey.

PICTURES

OVER DOOR TO CHAPEL:

After POLIDORO DA LANCIANO (*c.*1515–65)
The Holy Family with St Catherine and the Infant St John

LEFT OF CHAPEL DOOR:

GIOVANNI DOMENICO FERRETTI (1692–1766)
The Last Supper
In 1755 Walpole wrote to Horace Mann in Florence about the Chapel, 'If you can pick us up a tolerable Last Supper, ... we will say many a mass for the repose of your headaches'. This was the result.

RIGHT OF CHAPEL DOOR:

ELIZABETH CHUTE (d. 1913)
The Chapel, 1860

WALL OPPOSITE WINDOW:

? SPIRIDIONE ROMA (1737–87)
The Vyne Chapel
Perhaps intended to give John Chute an idea of how the Chapel would appear with Roma's decorations, although it does not show them as executed.

WALL OPPOSITE CHAPEL DOOR:

ENGLISH
Philip Chute of Appledore

FURNITURE

Settee, ebony with cane seat, Javanese

The four hall-chairs, oak, with vase-shaped splats are

English, *c.*1765, probably by France and Bradburne and bear an early version of the Chute crest.

The mahogany table is English, *c.*1750–60.

ALONG NEAR WALL:

The truncheons were used by the Special Constables of East Sherborne during the Corn Law disturbances of the 1840s.

SCULPTURE

The carved stone head from a Holy Trinity, *c.*1520–30, represents God the Father.

THE CHAPEL

The Chapel is of a magnificence not recorded outside the royal palaces of Tudor England, although its original arrangement and satellite rooms have changed. It probably extended originally into the present Ante-Chapel. To the right of the east window a door on the south wall may have led to the vestry, in which the 1541 inventory lists altar plate, cloths and vestments. At first-floor level Lord Sandys's closet, for attendance at Mass, occupies part of the present gallery over the Ante-Chapel. Lady Sandys's closet was possibly over the

The Chapel

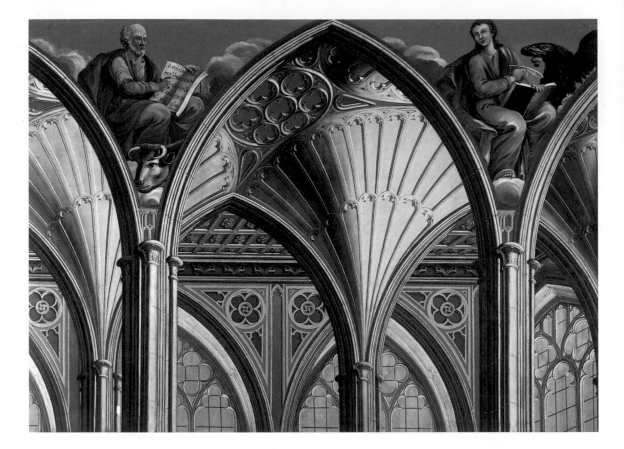

Detail of the north wall of the Chapel with its illusionistic Gothic vaulting and figures of St Luke and St Mark painted by Spiridione Roma, 1769–71

vestry, with an opening which is apparent in the masonry. The north wall of the Chapel would also have had windows above the ground floor. It is likely that the Sandys chapel replaces the earlier Chantry on or near the present site. Although the moulded decoration on the ceiling is similar to the sixteenth-century work, it may have been put up during late seventeenth-century repairs. The panelling at the east ends of the north and south walls is late seventeenth- or early eighteenth-century, and so may have been put up by Edward Chute.

In 1755 Horace Walpole suggested that the walls be painted in a Gothic pattern, with a closet with a screen in the same pattern. Considerable changes were made by John Chute, who in 1769 employed Spiridione Roma (1737–87) to provide *trompe-l'oeil* paintings on canvas for the upper parts of the south and north walls; these incorporated Gothic arcades and, in the spandrels, angels and the Four Evangelists. Roma also provided a painted curtain decoration for the west screen wall of the gallery. In 1998 the National Trust removed the canvases from Lord Sandys's closet and returned them to their mid-eighteenth-century arrangement above the stalls of the Chapel. A very rare Tudor decorative scheme was revealed on the north and south walls of the first-floor closet.

Wiggett Chute removed the Roma canvases to the gallery, rearranged the floor tiles, and added the woodwork beneath the middle window at the east end. The screen above the entrance to the Chapel was bought by Wiggett from the Music Room in Windsor Castle.

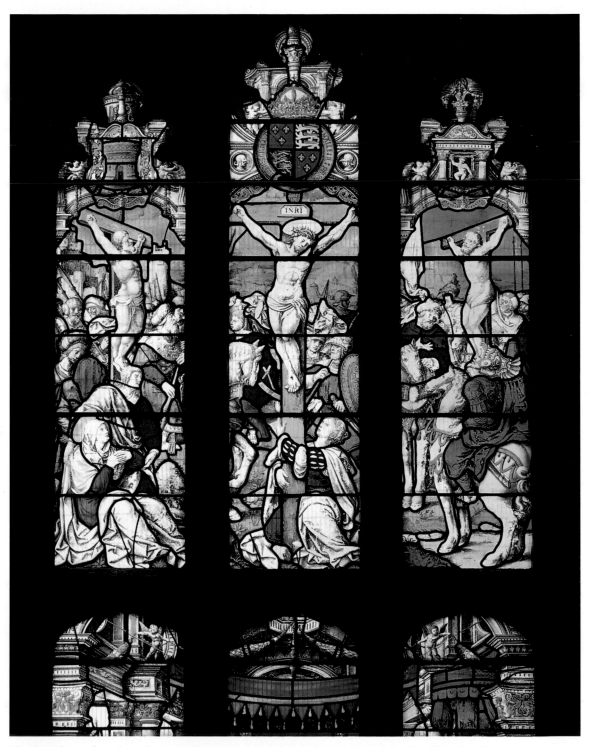

The Crucifixion; from the early sixteenth-century stained glass in the central window of the Chapel

WOODWORK

The stalls are among the last of a superb series of stalls made in early Tudor England: St George's Chapel, Windsor (1478–85), and Henry VII's Chapel in Westminster Abbey (*c*.1512) are the most elaborate examples. The stalls at The Vyne are close in style to those made for the Lady Chapel of Winchester Cathedral for Prior Silkstede, before 1524, although probably by a different workshop. They appear to be largely unaltered, except for the addition of coat or cassock pegs on the buttresses between the seats of the stalls. The bosses of the canopy and its frieze are decorated with heraldry, with royal devices and those of the Sandys and Bray families most prominent. The frieze incorporates running plant motifs with naked cherubs, which show the latest fashion for classical ornament; the Gothic decoration of the stalls is more conservative.

STAINED GLASS

The early sixteenth-century stained glass now in the east windows rivals that commissioned by Henry VIII for King's College Chapel, Cambridge, made in 1515–17 and 1526–47. For brilliance of colour and jewel-like clarity, it has no match in England.

TOP ROW: *The Passion of Christ*

RIGHT TO LEFT: *The Carrying of the Cross* and *The Meeting with St Veronica; The Crucifixion; The Resurrection*

BOTTOM ROW, CENTRE: *The young Henry VIII with his name saint, St Henry of Bavaria*

LEFT: *Queen Catherine of Aragon kneeling with St Catherine*

RIGHT: *Queen Margaret of Scotland, Henry VIII's sister, with St Margaret of Antioch*

The commission of the stained glass for the Chapel of the Holy Ghost, Basingstoke, and the tiles for the Tudor house, now brought together in the Chapel, reveal Sandys as an important patron of foreign craftsmen at a time when a new mercantile élite in the great ports of northern Europe was encouraging a growing trade in luxury goods and ideas between England, Flanders, Germany and Italy.

David Joris, a glazier from Bruges who was

A Flemish fool. The Chapel tiles were imported from Antwerp in the early sixteenth century

trained in Antwerp, was one of a group of ten glaziers that were taken into Sandys's service at Calais early in 1522 and came with him to England. They stayed at The Vyne for only a few weeks, probably making preparatory drawings, before Sandys had to return to Calais to prepare for the Emperor Charles V's visit to England. Bernard van Orley (*c*.1491/2–1541), court painter to the Regents of the Netherlands, may have been the chief designer of the Chapel glass, although he is unlikely to have actually painted it. At Brussels he supervised the weaving of tapestries for the Sistine Chapel in Rome from Raphael's famous cartoons (now on loan to the Victoria & Albert Museum). Certainly, the monumental figure of St Margaret of Antioch and the delicate blue-green landscapes in the upper windows suggest a close scrutiny of the cartoons, and a departure from the stylistic conventions of fifteenth-century Flemish panel painting, in which van Orley had been trained. The rich abundance of ornament on the fantastical, open loggia structure in the lower scenes remains traditionally Flemish, although indebted to north Italian prints, while the architecture itself is Italian in inspiration.

At first sight, the glass seems to be an exact fit, but closer inspection reveals it to have been cut down at the top of some of the lights; it is certainly not in its original state. Although the presence of royal figures sometimes prevented glass being destroyed during the Reformation, it is unlikely that the windows would have remained untouched through the religious upheavals of the sixteenth and seventeenth centuries. The most recent research by Hilary Wayment suggests that the windows were originally part of a larger cycle commissioned by Sandys for the Holy Ghost Chapel, Basingstoke, in the 1520s, when he was refounding the chantry and building the Holy Trinity Chapel there. In 1524 Sandys shipped glass direct from Flanders for the Holy Ghost Chapel, which included more scenes than are now at The Vyne, possibly making a complete cycle of the lives of Christ and the Virgin. Other fragments from the cycle survive in the churches of St Michael, Basingstoke, and Woolbeding, West Sussex. Portraits of Sandys and his wife as donor figures would probably have been included, as these fragments include parts of their personal arms.

The glass may have been removed from the Holy Ghost Chapel during the Civil War, when lead was stripped from its roof. It could have been placed in the Chapel by Edward Chute, who owned The Vyne from 1685 to 1722, as the arms of Chute impaled by Keck, marking the union of Edward Chute and Katherine Keck, appear in the top left-hand window. However, in the early seventeenth century some restoration took place, which suggests that it may have been installed here in the 1630s during the last years of Sandys's ownership. At this period Archbishop Laud was encouraging the enrichment of churches, and new vestments and other chapel textiles incorporating the Sandys arms from this period survive (now in the Victoria & Albert Museum). The glass was last releaded by Sir Charles Chute in the 1940s.

If the glass is a later introduction, what was here originally? Sandys may have had areas of clear glass, including a less ambitious cycle of small-scale biblical scenes and much scattered heraldry. Some of the heraldic fragments now in the Ante-Chapel and those given to St Michael's church, Basingstoke, by Sir Charles Chute, may have been part of this scheme.

TILES

In the early sixteenth century tiles were regularly imported from Antwerp by wealthy merchants.

Cardinal Wolsey had floor tiles from Antwerp at The More, his manor house in Hertfordshire, in the 1520s, and 'Flemish pavyinge tiles of grene and youllow' were ordered in the 1530s for Hampton Court and Christ Church, Oxford. Although such tiles were made in Flanders, their design and technology were largely in the hands of Italians at this period. The tiles at The Vyne are closest in style to the floor of square and hexagonal tiles commissioned in 1532 from the potter Petrus Frans van Venedigen (ie 'from Venice') for Herckenrode Abbey near Hasselt, and now in the Royal Museums, Brussels.

The tiles are glazed in four colours: lemon yellow (derived from antimony), cobalt blue, orange (made from antimony and iron), and bright green (from copper). Their motifs are Flemish adaptations of various Italian sources, such as coins, prints and manuscripts. They comprise classical and contemporarily dressed heads in profile and full face; animals and birds; fruit and foliage; and geometrical figures. Among the profile heads is the most famous image, which is often said to be of Federigo da Montefeltro, Duke of Urbino, after the portrait by Piero della Francesca (Uffizi, Florence), because of the hooked nose, but this is unlikely. One head is unquestionably Flemish: the fool wearing an eared cap labelled 'SOTGE'. Like the Fool in *King Lear*, this character provided earthy wisdom at the Flemish Chambers of Rhetoric, or *Rederijkers*, which were part drama companies, part schools of oratory.

The tiles are first recorded in the Chapel in the eighteenth century. In the 1840s Wiggett Chute relaid them in their present position, having found them arranged rather indiscriminately in front of the altar.

THE TOMB CHAMBER

The Tomb Chamber may occupy the position of the former vestry for the Chapel. Richard Bentley had made a proposal for what Walpole called a 'little Gothic Columbarium' (a place for displaying antique pottery originally containing human ashes). But ultimately John Chute designed the Tomb Chamber himself as a suitable setting for the magnificent monument to his seventeenth-century ancestor Speaker Chute, which he probably also conceived.

The Tomb Chamber

The monument, or cenotaph, to the Speaker by Thomas Carter the Younger (d. 1785) is one of the noblest works of late eighteenth-century English sculpture. It comprises a tomb chest with fluted Ionic columns incorporating panels with coats of arms supporting a life-size figure of the Speaker reclining on a woven straw mattress. In 1780, four years after John's death, Mrs Lybbe Powys refers to it as still incomplete.

High humidity has caused the once hard polished surface of the monument to fail. Consequently, the surface now has the consistency of sugar and regret-tably, it is necessary to restrict the access to the Tomb Chamber.

STAINED GLASS

The two windows are partly filled by glass painted by John Rowell in 1730–1 after Van Dyck. The larger of the two painted glasses was mentioned in one of Rowell's first advertisements, published in 1733. John Chute purchased them from Rowell's widow after his death in 1756.

Visitors should now retrace their steps to the Ante-Chapel and complete their tour, leaving the room by the south door.

THE PARK AND ESTATE

The landscape around The Vyne has passed through a typical sequence of changes since the Middle Ages. Part of the medieval park was later turned over to farming, and formal gardens were created around the house in the sixteenth and seventeenth centuries. These were supplanted by the fashion for informal landscaping up to the very doors of the house in the eighteenth century. Finally, in the mid-nineteenth century, more farmland was enclosed, and farming methods and buildings were modernised.

The Sandys family took over a medieval park – an enclosed tract of land, usually held by royal grant, for hunting and supplying timber. Such parks needed a variety of terrain: copses for cover, open grazing land and water. As wooded and uncultivated land, they are frequently found beyond the edge of villages, so it is no surprise to find that the medieval park was centred on an area well to the north-east of the village of Sherborne St John, past the site of the present house and centred around what is now Vyne Lodge Farm, which stands east of the present road to Bramley. During the sixteenth century, lands to the west of this road, including the area around The Vyne, were incorporated into the park.

The end of the medieval park probably came about through the relative neglect of the estate during the century or so after William Sandys's death in 1540, perhaps because the family lived increasingly at Mottisfont (see p. 47). When much of the old parkland was leased out in 1608–9, perhaps it was already being turned to farmland, and it has remained so ever since. This left about 40 acres around the house as gardens and park; they lie mainly to the west of the Bramley–Sherborne road, though a few fields to the east were later returned to parkland; in a map survey of 1776 these contained a rabbit warren, an orchard and a hop ground. The

Vyne does not have a great park around it, like some sixteenth-century houses, and was never transformed by the landscape schemes of the eighteenth century.

A small, mid-eighteenth-century painting of Anthony Chute's dog 'Chalons' shows a parterre and bowling green beyond the present lake. There could have been a garden there as early as Tudor times, which then survived, perhaps with the addition of fountains or ponds, until the 1720s, only to disappear during John Chute's changes after 1754. It probably stood just outside the moat of the Tudor house, which originally stretched to the edge of the present lake. The long terraced bank across the lake to the west of the house may have been built to prevent water from flowing unmanaged over this area.

Speaker Chute created further gardens to the north-east of the house, incorporating a red-brick summer-house c.1635, which can be seen from the road. Either Chaloner Chute or one of his successors may have built the first walled garden here. In Anthony Chute's accounts of 1743 there is reference to a 'Long Garden Pond' (as well as a 'great' pond), perhaps a long canal typical of formal gardens in the later seventeenth and early eighteenth centuries.

John Chute appears to have removed most of the formal garden features, though he retained the large walled garden enclosure to the north-east of the house. He may have been responsible for the final enlargement of the lake to the form we see today. All this is recorded on the estate map of 1776. He is also said by Chaloner Chute the Historian to have cut walks in Morgaston Wood and erected the statue of a Druid there, perhaps with Walpole's encouragement. However, the details of John Chute's changes remain a mystery and are barely recorded in his letters or other papers. The Chinese

*The garden from the west in the 1750s, showing the
chinoiserie bridge designed by John Chute and beyond it
the summer-houses, one of which still survives. However,
this drawing by J. H. Müntz is a somewhat idealised view
(Strawberry Parlour)*

bridge over the lower part of the lake shown in the
Müntz view of the garden of 1756 may have been
one of his earliest improvements. Walpole attrib-
utes it to John Chute, though it could equally have
been the work of his brother Anthony.

Caroline Workman records a further step taken
about 1808 in breaking up the formality of the
garden and approaches. The path to the house from
the stableyard to the north-east was now extended
past the front of the house to run south and meet the
road just past the Vyne Farm, as appears on the 1829
map of the estate. This informal approach probably
made redundant the formal avenue of already

decaying elm trees running south-east from the
house. A formal drive was replanted here by Sir
Charles Chute early in the twentieth century.

William Wiggett Chute made great changes to
the estate, particularly during the 1840s, noting that
the 'property was divided into small occupations,
rented in some cases by tenants who lived at
Basingstoke, or elsewhere, there being no house on
their farms, and very few of the tenants had any
capital, or were able to pay their rents with any
regularity.' He therefore set about a radical programme of improvement in true interventionist,
nineteenth-century fashion, enclosing huge areas
with new iron fencing. He was responsible for
removing the last remaining outlying hamlets to
bring their occupants nearer the church and school
in the village; a new school and school-house were
built in 1848. His alterations were published in the
Journal of the Royal Agricultural Society and sum-

marised with typical confidence by the Rev. James Edward Austen-Leigh, who wrote to Wiggett Chute in 1874 of 'the enclosure of the common fields, the construction of roads, which opened up Bramley and many other parts of the world, the draining and the letting in air and sunshine to the dark places of the earth.'

Much of the estate is covered by heavy London clay, and this, with the relatively low-lying terrain, accounts for its tendency to become waterlogged. Wiggett Chute's sister Caroline noted in the early nineteenth century that there were ruts 'deep enough to bury me in'. Wiggett Chute declared that when the tracks were bad, 'it was possible to drive from the village to the Vyne, but it was impossible to go beyond the Vyne stables on wheels, giving rise to the old saying that "the Vyne was the last place made on earth, and that Beaurepaire was made after it".' The improvement of the roads around The Vyne is due to Wiggett Chute's efforts in the 1840s. The present Morgaston Road at the northern edge of Morgaston Wood was created to demarcate the estate of The Vyne from that of Beaurepaire after Wiggett Chute had swapped parcels of land with his neighbour, Mr Brocas.

In the immediate vicinity of the house, Wiggett Chute pulled down two sides of the stableyard in 1844. To the north of the stables, he turned a small walled kitchen garden into an open flower garden and reduced the larger walled garden that survives to this day by excluding the canal that runs along one side of it. He built the two lodges at the southern edge of the estate in the style of the seventeenth-century summer-house, which was then being used as a pigeon-house. More than £250 was spent on cleaning and deepening the lake; 23,282 cubic yards of mud were removed at a cost of 4d per yard. He built a new iron bridge over the lower part of the lake, on the foundations of the earlier bridge here; this was lost in a storm in 1986. The National Trust hopes to reinstate the bridge despite the great expense of conserving the surviving ironwork and rebuilding the bridge support.

The present estate of 452 hectares (1,120 acres) has been much reduced since the nineteenth century. The storms of 1987 and 1991 also removed important trees from the landscape, part of the fruits of a programme of planting by Chaloner Chute the Historian during the 1880s. His avenue of limes running northwards from the garden-house to the walled garden can still, however, be seen. Among other important features of the garden are the 600-year-old 'Hundred Guinea' Oak behind the summer-house, and the claret vines, which recall the origin of The Vyne's name and which are trained on formal pyramidal frames by the door to the Stone Gallery.

The herbaceous borders to the west of the house were designed by the National Trust in the 1960s for a long season of summer interest and were last replanted in 1996. Another focus of effort in recent years has been the Wild Garden. This was created by Sir Charles Chute around 1910, using William Robinson's principles of semi-natural planting. Since 1995 the Trust has added strong-growing perennials in a contemporary version of the same approach. Currently, a formal Edwardian flower garden is being created in the enclosed area in front of the summer-house, with clipped yew and box hedges and beds of mixed perennials, bulbs and annuals laid out in a Greek-cross plan inspired by the plan of the summer-house itself.

The summer-house was probably built in the mid-seventeenth century

WILLIAM SANDYS AND THE TUDOR HOUSE

EARLY HISTORY

There are many stories about how The Vyne got its name. According to one theory, the house is on the site of the Roman road station called Vindomis, mentioned in the *Itineraries* of Antonine. However, this was partly based on the mistaken identification of Roman Calleva with Reading; it is now thought to have been either possibly at Silchester or at the small town of Neatham, near Alton. Another story, in William Camden's *Britannia* of 1586, has it that the first vines grown in England were propagated here at the time of the Emperor Probus between AD 276 and 282. The Roman road from Winchester to Silchester passed close to the edge of the nearby Morgaston Wood as late as medieval times, but the first known reference to the site as 'The Vyne' is not until a medieval document of 1268.

The Vyne once formed part of the manor of Sherborne Cowdray, which belonged to the Fyffhide family. At the death of Sir William Fyffhide in 1362, it was described as 'a manor house of no value beyond the outgoings and the advowdson [right of patronage] of the chapel'. When it was rented by a certain Gregory of Basingstoke in 1369–70, 'the manor house of Sherborne Cowdray' had consisted of a 'hall, adjoining chambers and the grange and chapel at the house'. The Vyne first entered the Sandys family by marriage in 1386, but passed out of it in 1420, when Joanna, daughter of Walter Sandys, married William Brocas, the owner of the neighbouring estate of Beaurepaire.

In medieval times and down to the sixteenth century, the area now covered by the house and its immediate surroundings was often referred to as the 'Vyne Green'. Access paths probably reached it from the east and west, that is towards the present wings containing the Chapel on one side, and the Stone and Oak Galleries on the other. This suggests that a miscellany of buildings once stood here, including a small moated manor house, a chantry chapel founded in 1337, and other free-standing buildings, which were later incorporated or adapted into the large Tudor courtyard house. The gallery wing is not at right-angles to the main block, confirming that Sir William Sandys's vast additions to the house were constructed one range at a time. In addition, there is archaeological evidence of structures, possibly including a tower, just west of the present Gallery range. Within the house there are especially thick walls at the centre, enclosing the Staircase Hall and between the present Large Drawing Room and the Strawberry Parlour and Print Room. The cellars beneath the Vestibule and Staircase Hall and under the south front running east from here may all once have been part of the medieval house.

WILLIAM SANDYS

The manor of The Vyne was recovered from the Brocas family in 1488 by Sir William Sandys, and inherited in 1496 by his son, another William, who was then probably in his mid-twenties. During the last years of Henry VII's reign the second William Sandys established himself in Court circles and continued to hold senior positions when the young Henry VIII succeeded in 1509. He was appointed a Knight of the Body to the new King and entertained him at The Vyne in 1510. The visit was part of the King's 'gests', his summer progresses away from London and the royal houses of the Thames valley into the countryside, to other royal houses and frequently also to those of leading courtiers.

During the early years of Henry VIII's reign Sandys was frequently absent from the country on royal and other business, both in war and peace. He was Treasurer to the Marquess of Dorset during the military incursions into France from the English territory around Calais in 1512 and he became

Treasurer of Calais in 1517. In 1520 he was one of three chief commissioners involved in preparations for the meeting of Henry VIII and François I at the Field of Cloth of Gold. Great honours followed: in 1518 the Order of the Garter, and in 1523 a peerage as Baron Sandys of The Vyne. This latter was a prerequisite for his major appointment at Court, that of Lord Chamberlain in 1526.

The Lord Chamberlain was head of the King's Chamber, the upstairs royal quarters of the palace (as opposed to below stairs, under the Lord Steward) and he was responsible for the organisation of its staff. It was ostensibly an extremely powerful position with direct access to the King, but since the foundation of an inner group of courtiers, the Privy Chamber, about 1495, it had probably become more ceremonial in character. This is why, despite the fact that Sandys appears to have grown politically distant from Henry VIII by about 1530, he managed to keep his place at Court until his death in December 1540. The conservative Sandys seems to have opposed the reform of the Church undertaken by the King following his decision to seek divorce from Catherine of Aragon, though, like all leading courtiers, he benefited from the Dissolution of the Monasteries, acquiring the Augustinian priory of Mottisfont in Hampshire from the Crown. He

The Oak Gallery panelling includes the cipher and rose-sun badge of William, Lord Sandys and the fleur-de-lis and tower of Henry VIII and Catherine of Aragon respectively

played the rather dangerous game of absenting himself from Court at crucial times, often claiming to be ill, whilst corresponding freely with Chapuys, ambassador from Catherine's nephew, the Emperor Charles V. Through age and inclination, he remained a soldier-administrator, a Henrician courtier of the Wolsey era, alongside other great builders like Henry, Baron Marney of Layer Marney in Essex, and Sir Richard Weston of Sutton Place in Surrey. Yet he retained the personal confidence of the King, who visited The Vyne twice more, in 1531 and 1535, on the second of these visits bringing his new queen, Anne Boleyn.

In Shakespeare's *Henry VIII* the character of Sandys describes himself as an 'honest country lord', delivers a tirade against French fashions, and against France as a place of ill winds blowing disease to English shores. The evidence of Sandys's travels, responsibilities and patronage of the arts argue otherwise. He is one of the few courtiers of the period for whom we have evidence that adds up to a picture of some experience and discrimination in the latest fashions of building and the decorative arts. He was married to Margery, niece and co-heir of Sir Reginald Bray, a close associate of Henry VII. Bray is often credited with having a hand in the design of both the new abbey of Bath and St George's Chapel, Windsor, to which he left a munificent bequest for the building of a chantry chapel, completed after his death in 1503. In 1524 Sandys was to build his own chantry chapel, dedicated to the Holy Trinity, at the chapel of the Holy Ghost in Basingstoke, employing the most prominent Flemish glaziers to fill its windows with stained glass, and it was here that he chose to be buried in a richly carved tomb. As commissioner for the Field of Cloth of Gold in 1520, he was closely involved in devising and completing the temporary palace built for Henry VIII in the Pas-de-Calais, a building which paid due reference in its decoration to the latest fashions promoted by the King's chief guest, François I of France. And most unusually for a Tudor courtier, often forced by Court duties to direct building operations at a distance, after he acquired Mottisfont in 1536, he appears to have taken an acute interest in adapting it into a new house, staying near the site to oversee his works

The ruins of the Holy Ghost chapel, where Sir William Sandys founded a chantry chapel dedicated to the Holy Trinity; watercolour by Elizabeth Chute, 1876

there. The surviving fragments of Sandys's lavish decoration of The Vyne – carved stonework displayed in the Stone Gallery, the carved panelling of the Oak Gallery and the tiles of the Chapel which were probably recovered from the earlier house in the eighteenth century – also fit the picture of a man who was a discriminating and fashionable patron of the arts.

THE TUDOR HOUSE

To get a sense of what Sandys's house looked like is difficult because so few comparable buildings survive in anything like their original state. The size and extent of Cardinal Wolsey's Base Court at Hampton Court, which was to become Henry VIII's great palace by the Thames, is a useful point of reference. The survival here of a complete court-yard of Tudor lodgings and service buildings helps us imagine what we have lost at The Vyne, since Sandys commanded great power and resources and would certainly have sought to rival the greatest in the land under the King.

At what date Sandys began integrating the various medieval structures on the site is difficult to determine at present. Some of it may have been done in the earliest years of his ownership and probably in time for the royal visit of 1510. Work must

have been substantially completed between 1515 (when Wolsey, whose arms appear in the Oak Gallery, was made a Cardinal) and 1526 (by which time the King was estranged from Catherine of Aragon, whose device, the pomegranate, appears in the woodwork of the Oak Gallery and Chapel).

There are three major sources of information about the size and contents of Sandys's house. Firstly, a description of the house by John Leland, probably in 1542, little more than a year after Sandys had died:

The Vine by Basingstoke was also of the Ancient Landes of the Sannes but it was given out in Marriage to one of the Brokesses; and so remainid until the late Lorde Sannes afore he was made Baron recoverid it into his possession; at the tyme ther was no very great or sumptuous Maner Place, and was only conteinid within the mote. But he after so translatid and augmentid yt, and beside buildid a fair Base Court that at this time is one of the Principale Houses in all Hamptonshire.

Secondly, the full inventory drawn up in the first months of 1541, shortly after Sandys's death, which describes a large and well-furnished house of 57 named rooms; there were doubtless many more that were not mentioned because they were empty of goods worth listing. The inventory must, however, be used with care, because only a few of the rooms it describes still survive.

The third item is a depiction of the house in the background of a double portrait painted in the 1640s, during the last years of the Sandys's ownership of the house. The old-fashioned appearance of the house seems to confirm the lack of evidence of any major building works between the death of the 1st Lord Sandys in 1540 and the radical changes that were to take place about ten years after this portrait was painted. It shows the building from the east, with the altar end of the chapel prominent. Crucially, it demonstrates that the present, surviving body of the house was always the main centre of the important rooms. This central block stands a storey higher than the structures to the north, which undoubtedly made up the 'fair Base Court' that Leland describes and which ran down to what is now the lake on that side of the house. These lower buildings are shown gabled, as indeed the main body of the house may originally have been. There may also have once been prominent buildings on the other, south side between the two present projecting wings. The battlemented tower shown at the far left-hand corner of the building may be the structure whose massive foundations have recently been discovered west of the Gallery range (see p. 46).

Given this information and the clues from the present building, what can be determined about

The east end of William Sandys's great mansion; from a portrait of the 1640s (private collection)

the Tudor house? From Leland's description and the 1541 inventory reference to a 'chamber at the bridge foot', it was certainly in part, if not entirely, a moated site. It had at least two entrances, since the inventory speaks of a chamber over the 'outer gate-house' and another over the 'gate'. Recent archaeology has rediscovered what Wiggett Chute first found in 1843 when he drained the lake: the remains of a Tudor bridge in the lake, leading north–south, that is to say towards the portico front, so the southern end of this bridge may indeed have been the site of the outer gatehouse. The house certainly had important sequences of rooms on both lower and upper floors. However, as earlier buildings were probably accommodated in the new whole, The Vyne may not have had as regular a layout of courtyards as comparable houses of this period, such as Knole in Kent. Nor can we assume that it had the conventional Tudor plan of a great hall between the private, family areas on one side and the domestic services, such as kitchen, buttery and pantry, on the other. Only at certain points, like the Oak Gallery and Chapel, can the inventory descriptions be applied without doubt to surviving room spaces. Nevertheless, they can be used to build up a mental picture of a grand house.

The inventory begins with the Hall, decked only with five pieces of old hangings of green say (a fine-textured cloth resembling serge) and a side cupboard covered with an old carpet. The relative lack of furnishing and lack of care paid to this room may indicate it had survived from the earlier house, but fallen into disuse. If the hall of the old manor house stood at the centre of the main range, running north–south in the area of the present Vestibule and Staircase Hall with a small wing to the east (exactly the area with cellars), then it might have been preserved by Sandys as an entrance hall.

The parlour which follows in the inventory is, by contrast, elaborately furnished and hung with old, though still valuable, tapestry. We then pass to the 'Rose chamber' (perhaps named after Tudor roses used as part of its decoration) and rooms leading off it. The next reference, to a 'chamber over the buttery', suggests that the buttery (the storeroom for drink) may have been in the cellarage under the house, where it is also found in some comparable

Tudor houses. After passing through some rooms which appear to give on to the base court to the north, the inventory reaches the 'new' parlour, suggesting some distinction between an old part of the house and the new parts which Sandys had built; here the tapestry is described as 'new' and the bed may have been that made for the earliest royal visit, for it is decorated with Tudor roses and the pomegranate device of Catherine of Aragon.

When the inventory passes to the 'Great chamber over the parlour', we appear to move upstairs and there begins a remarkable series of rooms that are of considerable historical importance. In a circuit of rooms which twice comes back to the threshold of the great chamber, suites of rooms for the King and Queen are described as separated by a gallery, which is certainly the present Oak Gallery. The royal lodgings are lavishly decorated, the contents of the Queen's rooms being of somewhat higher value than the King's. The King's chamber, with its

bed of green velvet fringed with silver and gold, gives off the 'portcullis' chamber, which served as his great, or possibly guard, chamber. Both sovereigns have a pallet chamber for a body servant. This plan presumably dates from the visit of Henry VIII and Anne Boleyn in 1535. Indeed, having both sets of royal apartments together on the upper floor with a gallery as the channel of communication between them echoes the latest arrangements in the great royal palaces, such as Hampton Court.

Sandys and his wife may have subsequently used the royal lodgings, as the inventory records no other rooms for them, and both in the Queen's great chamber and her 'lying chamber' were hangings decorated with Sandys's arms. That the gallery of the inventory is indeed the present Oak Gallery, albeit slightly altered in its fenestration and the arrangement of the panelling, seems proved by the fact that it has no hangings, presumably in order to show the elaborate oak wainscotting. It is only minimally furnished with curtains and carpets to the windows, plus two other carpets, two small tables, a 'spanyshe folding chaire', and 'two small crepers of iron' for a fireplace.

The presence upstairs of a 'great dining chamber', the room that follows the Queen's lodging, suggests that it was the chief ceremonial room in the suite. The Tower chamber which follows could be the space over the present Dining Parlour, because, after three further small rooms off this, we arrive at closets for Lord and Lady Sandys 'over' and 'next to' the Chapel. These were certainly both on the upper floor, as it was usual in great houses for the household to hear Mass in the body of the Chapel and for the master of the house and his wife to hear it from closets above the Ante-Chapel and south of the Chapel respectively. Both these closets were comfortably furnished with tapestries; William Sandys's closet also had an altar in it, suggesting he might on occasion have heard private mass there. It is likely that the Chapel originally extended into the space now forming the Ante-Chapel, the latter forming the body of the Chapel and the present Chapel the choir and sanctuary. Surviving Tudor doorways (one now blocked) perhaps allowed the household to enter the Chapel from outside the house, or from rooms later demolished.

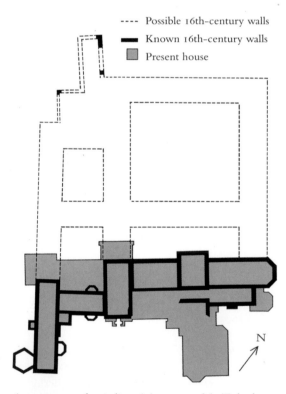

--- Possible 16th-century walls

— Known 16th-century walls

■ Present house

N

A recent survey has indicated the extent of the Tudor house

Henry VIII kneeling, with his patron saint, Henry II of Bavaria; from the Chapel stained glass commissioned by William Sandys

ments for priests, deacon and sub-deacon. The magnificent choir-stalls suggest an exceptional number of singers for a private chapel, and most significant among the music books listed are three 'pricksong books' for the singing of polyphonic music.

After a vestry, the inventory seems to pass via a gateway into the base court where there were rooms for the schoolmaster, cook and yeomen. Also here were a wardrobe of beds and an audit parlour. There appears to have been a series of rooms off another gallery, probably this time a covered walk giving on to the court (a similar arrangement was found at the great house of the King's brother-in-law, Charles Brandon, Duke of Suffolk, at Westhorpe in Suffolk). An armoury contained German breast- and back-plates, 'chasing staves' and javelins. There was also 'a pavilion conteyning iii chambers and a hall new with all their appurtenances esteemed and valued at £40', a reminder perhaps of Sandys's role at Court where such temporary pavilions were used at tournaments and jousts, and on ceremonial occasions like the Field of Cloth of Gold.

THE LATER SANDYS FAMILY

Although the adaptation of Mottisfont was unfinished at William Sandys's death, in subsequent years his descendants seem to have used that house as their main residence more extensively than The Vyne. However, his grandson Henry commemorated his marriage to the daughter of the 2nd Lord Windsor with an elaborately embroidered heraldic cushion cover, which is decorated with a pattern of vine leaves in honour of the house (now in the Victoria & Albert Museum). And Henry's son, the young William, 3rd Lord Sandys, entertained Elizabeth I at The Vyne in 1569, but a later, more famous visit by the Queen coincided with a severe downturn in the family fortunes. In February 1601 the 3rd Baron was fined £5,000 and imprisoned in the Tower for his part in the Earl of Essex's insurrection. It is likely that The Vyne was still temporarily in the hands of the Crown, when, in September of the same year, it was made ready for the French Ambassador, the Duc de Biron, and his

As early as the twelfth century the neighbouring manor of Sherborne Cowdray had its own chapel, which was re-endowed in 1337 by Sir Thomas de Cowdray as a chantry chapel, where a priest would say masses and pray for the souls of the deceased. William Wiggett Chute and his son, Chaloner, believed that this stood to the south of the house, across the present road to Bramley. But it is more likely that Sandys rebuilt the present Chapel on or near the site of the original chantry. A chantry 'at the Vyne' was suppressed in 1549, when such chapels and their priests were no longer permitted.

The chapel of The Vyne was certainly fully integrated with the rest of the house and served as a lavish private chapel. In fact, there is no recorded private chapel in early Tudor England as richly appointed as this outside the royal palaces. The inventory lists plate, altar-cloths, hangings and vest-

This mid-sixteenth-century embroidered cushion cover commemorates the marriage of William Sandys's grandson, Henry, with Elizabeth, daughter of the 2nd Lord Windsor. The vine leaves recall the origin of the house's name (Victoria & Albert Museum)

suite of 400, who were conducted to the house by Sir Walter Ralegh. The Queen, who stayed nearby at Basing House, the home of the Marquess of Winchester, came to visit him. The Vyne was clearly by this time a house lacking many basic furnishings. Hangings and plate had to be imported from the Tower and Hampton Court and, according to the chronicler John Stow, the house was fitted out with 'seven score beds and furniture, which the willing and obedient people of Hampshire, upon two days' warning had brought thither to lend the Queen'. Stow continues:

The Duke abode there four or five days all at the Queen's charges and for that time spent her more at the Vine than her own court spent at Basing: and her Majesty affirmed that she had done that in Hampshire that none of her ancestors ever did, neither that any prince in Christendom could do, that was, she had in her Progresse in her subjects' houses, entertained a royal ambassador, and royally entertained him.

The 3rd Lord Sandys died in 1623, when the title passed to his son William, and six years later to the latter's half-sister Elizabeth, who thus became Baroness Sandys in her own right. Her son, Colonel Henry Sandys, appears to have lived at the house. He fought for Charles I during the Civil War, and The Vyne was occupied by Parliamentary troops under the command of Sir William Waller in 1643 during the siege of Basing House. That Royalist stronghold, a brick and stone citadel built for Sir William Paulet, another courtier of Henry VIII, was relieved twice in two years before it finally fell to Parliamentary forces in October 1645. At times Basing was surrounded by thousands of troops, and the hundreds that sporadically relieved it would have marched quite close by The Vyne on the last stage of their journey from the Royalist base at Oxford to the north. Quartering troops and foraging for supplies for thousands of men must have drained the resources of this part of Hampshire.

Col. Sandys died after being wounded near Alresford in 1644, and some years later his son William was forced to sell the house. With this sale, the Sandys family's connections with The Vyne came to an end.

CHALONER CHUTE
AND JOHN WEBB

At the end of the siege of Basing House in 1645, one of those taken prisoner by the Parliamentary forces was the King's architect, Inigo Jones, then more than 70 years of age, who was reputedly stripped of his clothes and carried out in a sack. It is ironic that Jones's pupil and the heir to his classical architectural vision, John Webb, should have been employed at The Vyne by the man who was to become Speaker of the House of Commons during the Commonwealth. The new owner, Chaloner Chute, bought the house from the impoverished Sandys family in 1653. Chute was a lawyer famed for his even-handedness: when the bishops were impeached by Parliament in 1641, he was one of the counsel retained to defend them, and it was through his advice that the case was dropped. Chute was elected MP for Middlesex in 1656 but could not take his seat until re-elected two years later. On 27 January 1659 he was elected Speaker of the Commons to much general acclaim, but was forced to relinquish the post early in March for the sake of his health and died the following month.

Though a loyal servant of the Protectorate during its last difficult days under Richard Cromwell, it was believed that Chute looked to a restoration of the monarchy as the cure for the country's ills. Edward Hyde, later Earl of Clarendon and leading minister to Charles II, wrote just a few weeks after Chute's death: 'I am very heartily sorry for the death of the speaker, whom I have known well, and am persuaded he would never have subjected himself to that place if he had not entertained some hope of being able to serve the king.' Chute died in Chiswick, probably at the house called Sutton Court, owned by the Chapter of St Paul's Cathedral and sub-let to him. He was buried in St Nicholas's

Church, Chiswick, where he had been a church-warden many years before. In view of what was to happen at The Vyne, it is interesting that Chute's suburban house was within the belt of Thames-side villas which were central to the development of the villa form in the seventeenth and eighteenth centuries.

What sort of house did Chute envisage? It was to be radically different from the Tudor Vyne, as he

(Right) Chaloner Chute, who bought The Vyne in 1653 and commissioned John Webb to transform it

demolished about two-thirds of the old building and built the north-west tower and the present range to the east of it to tidy up a façade originally forming part of the Tudor courtyards. Many patrons of the time attempted to transplant from London into their country estates a style of classical architecture that took individual features from source books, but eschewed the order and decorative restraint that the Jonesian style demanded. More unusual were those buildings which did continue the dialogue with the Antique and the Italian Renaissance initiated by Jones. John Webb was the champion of the latter.

Webb's study of Palladian villa architecture resulted in houses such as Lamport in Northamptonshire, contemporary with The Vyne and built for Sir Justinian Isham. Here Webb fronted a Tudor house with a small, five-bay villa façade, which employed the architectural language of Jones's Banqueting House in Whitehall. At The Vyne, he was to attempt something more radical, though only the bare bones of his overall idea are now recoverable. What quite emphatically does exist, however, is the striking external feature that Webb was to incorporate into several of his houses – the portico. Projecting from the building, the Corinthian portico at The Vyne is unique for the 1650s in England. Indeed, until Horace Walpole's *Anecdotes of Painting* (1762–80), it was attributed to Inigo Jones, who had pioneered the form at St Paul's, Covent Garden, in the 1630s.

Chute may have been introduced to Webb through a family connection. As his second wife, he married in 1650 Dorothy, the widow of the 13th Lord Dacre. Her stepson Francis was to commission Webb to work at Chevening in Kent in 1655. Three documents (now in the Hampshire Record Office) which are effectively contracts between Chaloner Chute and the mason Edward Marshall, record work completed at The Vyne between March 1655 and the end of 1656. Webb used Marshall on several commissions, notably in 1656 at Syon for the 10th Earl of Northumberland, and, in the 1660s, on Northumberland House, and they wrote a joint report on the state of St Paul's Cathedral, three years before the Great Fire. The work on The Vyne was to be performed 'well and workmanlike' by Marshall 'according to such directions as shall be from time to time given him by the surveyor', a reference to Webb. It seems that Webb frequently used London masons like Marshall on projects in the country because he doubted whether local craftsmen had the level of expertise needed to achieve the fine detail of the urban classical style. In addition, there are two drawings of the capitals for the portico by Webb in his Book of Capitals, now at Chatsworth. One of these is marked 'for Mr Chute at the vine'.

The Marshall documents are in no sense full building accounts, but they suggest that by the time this phase of the work began in the spring of 1655 what was not required of the old Tudor house was already disappearing, leaving only the main block extant. Work was contracted to be finished by August of the same year 'if he bee not hindered by the Bricklayers or Carpenters'. The documents record work carried out in stone, and it was this which essentially gave The Vyne its new, classical character. The battlements were coped in stone at two shillings per foot. The windows were newly set up and cut with square heads (thus removing all the old arched heads to the lights and almost certainly at the same time regularising the window arrangement generally, although casements were retained) at a cost of £1 16s each. The two Corinthian capitals

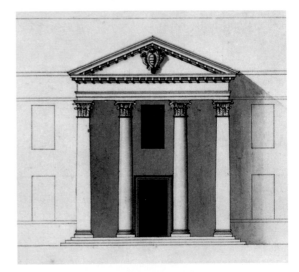

Webb's portico was the first on an English country house; detail from a drawing by Henry Flitcroft

of the central pillars of the portico, in Burford stone, cost, in materials and workmanship, £13 apiece, each of the two corner pier capitals £11. The column shafts are in brick, rendered in stucco, and so do not appear in the accounts. The bases of the pillars were made of Portland stone at a cost of £5 10s each. This sensitivity to the different qualities of native stones and their suitability for different purposes was part of Jones's legacy. The Chute arms on the portico, also in Burford stone, cost £3.

Within the house there was much moving around of old paving in some of the older areas of the house, including the hall, 'below the chapel' and in the cellar, but much new paving was also brought in; Portland for the paving of the portico, and a total of 434 feet of black and white stone, in addition to 40 other black and white stones, for the great staircase. Much expensive stone was laid as hearths to newly decorated rooms. Nine old stone doorcases and six old fireplaces of stone were taken down and 'repaired' (probably recut). Ten new chimneypieces are mentioned, including two in white marble and six in Portland stone. Among these are probably the white marble chimneypiece in the Oak Gallery, the most unambiguously Webb in style, with garlands descending either side of a cartouche placed amid a broken pediment. Also upstairs, but moved from what is now the Tapestry Room into the present Library, is a stone chimneypiece with flanking engaged columns arranged with tiers of palm leaves. The Chute arms appear in a cartouche at the centre. One stone chimneypiece downstairs, in the Saloon, could possibly be one of the refashioned pieces mentioned in the documents. The chimneypieces of the Library, Oak Gallery and the Large Drawing Room, albeit the latter was created from an overmantle frame, all represent a rare survival of pre-Restoration design which relates to earlier work of Inigo Jones, of whom John Webb was a pupil.

It is, however, difficult to visualise the overall character and plan of the new house Chute commissioned. Was it even finished to his specifications, given the brief time available before his death in 1659? It is also unclear when Chute took up residence at The Vyne. For the majority of this period he appears to have been living at Belhus in Essex.

Webb designed ten new chimneypieces for The Vyne, probably including the marble palm-decorated fireplace now in the Library, and the overmantel now in the Large Drawing Room. This drawing was made about 1830, when both were still in the Tapestry Room

No inventory of The Vyne survives from the seventeenth century, but the 1754 inventory may record at least some of the internal arrangements arrived at a century earlier, as no major building works are recorded before the mid-eighteenth century. Webb's emphatic portico as a new entry to the house appears to promise a distinctly classical house within.

Webb had helped to revive the ancient Roman practice of great pillared halls leading to lower- and upper-floor rooms carefully proportioned in relation to each other and linked by complex and innovative double-flight staircases. He used this sequence in his compact villa designs, notably at the lost house of Gunnersbury in Middlesex, but also at Belvoir

Castle, Leicestershire, begun in 1655, at exactly the same time as The Vyne. At Belvoir a hall with eight columns runs through the middle of the house at right-angles to its main axis. The similar space at the centre of The Vyne suggests that Webb may have planned something like this here. Indeed, in his continual reference back to Webb when redesigning the central space in the 1750s and 1760s, John Chute often returned to the idea of an eight-columned hall.

One thing, however, is clear from the documents. The 1754 inventory describes the central space now occupied by John Chute's Vestibule and Staircase Hall as 'The Stone Hall and Stairs'. Clearly, the paving which Marshall supplied was placed here. So it is most likely that in rearranging this space, John Chute removed a pre-existing staircase, which in itself had probably been the first grand stairs in this house. Indeed, the account of November 1655, which lists what has been achieved thus far, corroborates this. It states that most of Marshall's work is complete save for the crest at the front (ie on the portico) and the watertables (projecting mouldings) 'from the Angle of the Portico to the Tower next to the Chappell, & on the backside of the House *from the further Angle of the Staircase* [my italics] to the corner of the old building'. This seems to refer to two parallel stretches of moulding, one on the north front, from the portico to the tower of what is now the Dining Parlour, and the other on the south (called the 'backside') from the small projecting angle of the Staircase Hall to the angle of the east wing.

Two features in the park also appear to date from the Webb period. The gate-piers that now flank the entrance from the south, on the road between the village of Sherborne St John and Bramley, are sometimes attributed to Webb himself. His contemporary work at Lamport included gate-piers, also rusticated to encourage moss and lichen as 'for the gathering of some greene it is not amisse, it being a symptome of Antiquity'. The other structure often associated with Webb is the red-brick summer-house that stands to the north-east of the house. Views of the house by Müntz in the 1750s suggest that it was once one of a pair. A raised platform in the lawn to the west of the surviving pavilion may be the site of this, but its existence remains speculative, as it is not shown on a map of 1776. A recent archaeological survey suggests it was built some twenty years before Webb's augmentation of the Tudor house. Its earliest use is uncertain, though it originally had an upper floor. By the eighteenth century, it was in use as a summer-house.

Finally, Chute's transformation of The Vyne is eloquent about the new house's classical identity, in his respect for its setting. When we consider that the access from the north was preserved, and stonework apparently added to the top of the old Tudor bridge across the stream there, it is perhaps not too fanciful for us to evoke the image of a Palladian villa on the Brenta in the Veneto. This image is reinforced by today's view, across what later became a lake; it is a panoramic view which is centred on the portico entrance.

Chute's immediate successors seem to have undertaken no major structural works. His son, also called Chaloner, outlived him by only seven years, leaving a son, again named Chaloner, to inherit at the age of ten under the guardianship of his grandmother, the Speaker's widow, Dorothy. The period until Chaloner III's death in 1685 was dominated by court actions between him and his grandmother over his legacy, the management of the estate and the maintenance of the younger grandchildren. These disputes probably resulted in most of the furnishings and pictures being given to Dorothy's favourite grandson, Thomas, who settled at Pickenham in Norfolk about 1700. Chaloner's other brother, Edward, inherited The Vyne in 1685, living until 1722.

During Edward Chute's tenure, the house was evidently kept in repair, since the initials of Edward and his wife Katherine, *née* Keck, appear on some of the rainwater hoppers. The arms of Chute impaled by Keck were added to the stained glass of the Chapel, indicating restoration of the Tudor work, or more likely that the windows were inserted into the Chapel at this time.

Some items of furniture from the early eighteenth century survive in the house, as do the set of Soho tapestries depicting Indian subjects now hanging in the Tapestry Room, though these could have been purchased after Edward Chute's time.

JOHN CHUTE AND 'STRAWBERRY GOTHIC'

In the history of eighteenth-century English architecture and interior design, The Vyne holds an important place, because from 1754 to 1776 it belonged to John Chute (1701–76), a close friend of Horace Walpole. Chute was a member of the 'Committee of Taste' that supervised the enlargement and decoration of Strawberry Hill, Walpole's villa near Twickenham and a landmark in the history of the Gothic Revival. The association with Walpole is preserved to this day in the Strawberry Parlour at The Vyne. This room, with its dark panelling and collection of Chute drawings and projects on the walls, evokes the Walpole circle's enthusiasm for antiquarianism.

Yet in no sense did Chute attempt to imitate Strawberry Hill at The Vyne; indeed, he often rejected Walpole's advice. In the London of their day, fashionable architecture and interior design became increasingly dominated by the classical revival of Robert Adam, which determined every detail of the interior. Despite the fame and influence of the Gothic Revival interiors at Strawberry, the Walpole circle by contrast had no prescriptive rules about style. What they shared was an enthusiasm for historic and curious objects which could best be displayed in suitably evocative 'Romantic' interiors. In their world, Classical and Gothic often therefore sat comfortably alongside each other; the particular mixture was determined by the history of the place and the interests of its past owners. Chute's Gothic Revival additions to The Vyne derived a sense of authenticity from the 'Tudor Gothic' of Sandys's time, but also respected the history of the house as a whole.

John Chute was the youngest of Edward Chute's ten children and, as he was unlikely to inherit the family estates, spent many years travelling in Italy. He was never to marry, but surrounded himself with younger men, including his handsome, wealthy and deaf cousin, Francis Whithead, whose portrait in pastels after Rosalba Carriera still hangs in the Further Drawing Room. In Italy the two inseparable cousins were called the 'Chutheads'. Chute was practically a generation older than the 23-year-old Walpole (like Chute, a younger son with leisure on his hands) and the future poet, Thomas Gray, when he met them in Florence in 1740. Chute and Walpole were temperamentally very different. Walpole was energetic, impatient, incisive and a political intriguer. Chute was slow, cautious, not a political animal beyond serving as the Sheriff of

John Chute; by Gabriel Mathias, 1758 (Large Drawing Room). He holds a plan for gothicising the south front. In the background is Webb's portico

Francis Whithead, who accompanied his cousin, John Chute, on the Grand Tour in 1740; pastel after Rosalba Carriera

Hampshire, and prone to disastrous interventions in his friends' affairs. During the latter part of his time in Italy, he was already suffering from the gout and deafness that plagued him for the rest of his life; gout condemned him to a diet of milk and turnips.

Chute's prospects were transformed by the death of his brother Francis in 1745, which made him heir presumptive to The Vyne. He returned home the following year, despite commenting from Rome that he was 'not able to find the least comfort in being one horrid step nearer to a mouldering estate'. In subsequent years, relations with his elder brother Anthony, owner of the house, were not good; certainly Walpole was convinced that John could yet be disinherited. On the other hand, Chute appears to have taken a serious interest in The Vyne and particularly its collections. In 1753 he wrote to Anthony from London urging him to obtain a set of plaster busts for the Oak Gallery; three are now displayed in the Stone Gallery. It is also likely that he secured from Italy the ebony casket with *pietra dura* panels now in the China Room, which probably arrived at the house in the late 1740s.

Anthony Chute remains a rather shadowy figure, whose main interest seems to have been his horses. He was elected MP for Yarmouth on the Isle of Wight in 1734, twelve years after he had succeeded to The Vyne on the death of his father. According to Walpole, he was responsible for putting sash-windows into the north front, since Webb's square-headed windows of the 1650s would have originally contained casements. Many objects in the house today tell of Anthony Chute's taste. Accounts from the London furniture makers Vile and Cobb record purchases in 1752–3, including a set of six chairs at 19s each (four now survive) and eight leather-covered benches each priced at £3 12s. At the same time he commissioned from William Vile the stand for the 'stone cabinett' already mentioned. The round mirror with the head of Apollo at its centre hung in the Dining Parlour at his death in 1754, and has been returned there. He also acquired many of the eighteenth-century fittings, such as the pier-glasses between the windows of the Saloon (then known as the 'Great Hall') and the grates and andirons of several fireplaces. He certainly had the Portland stone paving laid in the Stone Gallery, or the 'greenhouse', as it continued to be called.

John Chute acted with characteristic caution on inheriting The Vyne in 1754, when he was already deeply involved with Walpole's projects for Strawberry Hill. Walpole had first leased the small, late seventeenth-century house which he turned into his 'little Gothic castle' of Strawberry in 1747. In 1751 he formed the 'Committee on Taste' around himself, including the architect Richard Bentley and Chute. Initially, Walpole culled ideas for the revived Gothic from the works of the early topographers of medieval buildings. Only later did they test their findings against the originals, sometimes being surprised by the scale and materials of what they found. In 1752 Walpole and Chute travelled all over Kent and Sussex; among the 'thousand sketches' they made were of sites such as Battle Abbey and Herstmonceux Castle. Under Walpole's firm control, Chute was largely responsible for the external elevations of the extensions to Strawberry Hill made up to 1763. The great majority of the preparatory drawings for these are in his hand.

Chute is usually credited with designing the fireplace and possibly the canopies and ceiling of the Gallery, decorated in 1761–3. He was also responsible for much of the interior of the Tribune, or Cabinet, designed to house Walpole's rarest curiosities. Quasi-religious ceremonies marked the completion of each room: 'I am expecting Mr. Chute to hold a chapter on the cabinet', Walpole wrote, '. . . a bargeload of niches, window-frames and ribs is arrived.' Chute's last work at Strawberry was a small, octagonal, fan-vaulted chapel in the garden, built in 1772–3. At Strawberry Hill, Chute followed Walpole's direction in creating a house that was curious, labyrinthine, a kind of visual equivalent of Walpole's Gothic novel, *The Castle of Otranto* (1765). In other architectural commissions, such as Donnington Grove in Berkshire (1763–5), he applied Gothic more sparingly, showing what one historian has called 'a classical purist's sense of style and proportion', in marked contrast to the asymmetry of Strawberry Hill. By the 1760s, a similar sensitivity to different traditions was manifest at The Vyne.

When Chute inherited The Vyne, Walpole responded with customary energy and enthusiasm, seeing it as an opportunity to extend the Straw-

The 'lattimo' ware plates in the China Room feature views of Venice and were bought by John Chute while on the Grand Tour

berry Committee's work. He compiled an *Inventionary* in 1755 with a list of proposed alterations, to be carried out at a cost of £5,000. It suggested the placing over the doors of the 'great parlour' (the present Drawing Room) portraits of himself, Gray, Bentley, and the now deceased Francis Whithead, a true 'Strawberry' circle of Chute's friends. He gave Chute important pieces of furniture from his own family collection, probably including the William Kent table with the arms and motto of Sir Robert Walpole worked into the top, made of scagliola. By 1757, however, Walpole was lamenting that Chute was not changing the house quickly enough; 'I have done advising', he wrote petulantly to George Montagu, 'as I see Mr. Chute will never execute anything.' He took to petty complaints, such as despairing of the dampness of The Vyne, which was frequently cut off by floods in bad weather. In 1759 he begged Chute to leave the house for a while lest he should 'die of mildew'.

The friendship between Chute and Walpole in fact never faltered, but Chute was not to be rushed. He also moved carefully because he was often embarrassed for money, particularly during the 1760s; in 1760 he was forced to sell his house in Tilney Street, Mayfair, for £3,000. In 1762 he mortgaged The Vyne and sold outlying estates. By 1765 his finances had improved sufficiently for him to buy and furnish a house in Charles Street, off Berkeley Square. From 1754 he was helped in the visual realisation of his projects at The Vyne by the artist Johann Heinrich Müntz, who spent six months here in 1755, before helping to establish a printing press at Strawberry Hill. Müntz's drawing and watercolour of The Vyne from the north-west present the house in an idealised way, somewhere between the reality of the building as it stood in the mid-1750s and Chute's vision for it. A fanciful three-storey tower, similar to that on the northwest of the house, is added to the south-west corner to give the building the four-square appearance of a brick, classical villa with a portico at the centre of a symmetrical north front. The unsymmetrical Gothic Chapel wing is conveniently shrouded by a screen of trees. The north front of the house was, however, the one side that Chute does not seem to have been interested in altering to any great extent.

This was due partly to his respect for Webb's work and partly because it now became the back, or garden, side to the house. A great number of surviving drawings show alternative ideas for the other three façades.

Gabriel Mathias's portrait of Chute provides a key to understanding the double-edged character of what he sought to do: he is shown standing in front of the disembodied portico, which symbolises the house's antiquity. In his hand, however, he holds a view of a proposal for the south front, which is classical in its symmetry but Gothic in its embellishments. Chute was never to resolve the conflicting instincts he had about the exterior, and a mass of surviving drawings reveal a constant turning between classical and Gothic styles. Gothic remained his instinctive choice: drawings of the south front with Gothic embellishments were rapidly executed with great confidence. But classi-

cal solutions, and particularly classical details, were more carefully drawn, as if his rational instincts were overcoming his imaginative ones.

Chute's drawings have often been described as dry, even 'anorexic' in character. It is certainly a draughtsmanship governed by the ruler and the compass; there is rarely any wash applied to give a sense of place or shadow to his elevations. Perhaps Müntz's views were intended to supply this. None of Chute's ideas for the house is as finished in execution as the finest of his drawings for Strawberry Hill, and they are rarely worked out consistently in relation to each other. No drawing is accompanied by careful measurements. Even in his Gothic solutions, he retains the square heads to the windows. What gives certain schemes their Gothic character is mainly the pinnacles and battlements of the skyline; the classical symmetry of the south front is always preserved. It was very much therefore a

The Vyne from across the Lake; by J. H. Müntz, a Swiss artist much patronised by John Chute's friend Horace Walpole. Müntz spent six months at The Vyne in 1755. The far right-hand tower was probably never built

process of experimentation with different forms of architectural 'dress' as alternative ways of clothing the old building. The Vyne was already a substantial house that Chute had no wish to enlarge; it was quite different from Strawberry Hill, which grew into its pleasing asymmetry by a series of additions to a small old house.

Along with surviving evidence of decoration and furnishings, inventories taken in 1754 and 1776, at the deaths of Anthony and John Chute, allow us to visualise the changes that John brought about to the interior. The rooms along the north front in *enfilade* remained the main rooms of reception. About 1768, the suite of three rooms in the north-west corner was hung with crimson and white brocatelle, bought in Genoa at a cost of 18s 6d a yard. He is also likely to have inserted the rococo papier-mâché ceilings in these rooms. They are among the most delicate of their kind in England, paralleled by similar work at nearby Stratfield Saye. In this suite, Chute gathered objects from his Italian travels.

Elsewhere in the house, Chute sought to underline its age and distinguished history. He was known in the Walpole circle as an expert in genealogy, the 'Strawberry King-at-Arms' as Sir Horace Mann dubbed him. The Oak Gallery, with its record in the panelling of the great men of Henry VIII's time, was already a picture gallery in 1754, hung with portraits of people associated with the house and figures from English history. By 1776 the room had been filled with more furniture and curiosities. Below, the Stone Gallery was lined with chairs and, in winter, with orange and myrtle trees in tubs. Given his awareness of The Vyne's Tudor origins, Chute was probably responsible for inserting over the fireplace the sixteenth-century terracotta roundel, which is similar to those made by the Italian Giovanni da Maiano for Cardinal Wolsey's Hampton Court in 1521. He could have obtained this roundel when the Tudor 'Holbein' gateway in Whitehall was demolished in 1759–60.

In the inventories of 1754 and 1776, the Saloon is described as the 'Great Hall'. The eighteenth-century owners used this term historically, for the contents suggest that it did not serve as a conventional eighteenth-century hall or vestibule. Rather,

The Genoese crimson and white brocatelle was hung in the Large Drawing Room about 1768

it was furnished as a comfortable sitting-room in 1776, with a large Wilton carpet, card-tables, a sofa and chairs, and check curtains. It was important to convey a sense of the past here, as this was the first of the sequence of rooms east of Chute's new staircase that culminated in the Tudor Chapel, a place of supreme reverence for the Walpole circle. This sense of venerable age is clear from Mrs Lybbe Powys's description of the 'Great Hall' given in 1780, which records Chute's recent redecoration: 'The room we dined in, of a vast length, is painted dark blue, small old panels, in each of which is a gold star, the cornice gilt. It has not a bad appearance in a house of that antiquity.' The panelling survives but is now stripped of its paint. The stars (actually roses) that gave it the name of 'Starred Hall' in the nineteenth century have been reintroduced. The centre of the ceiling was raised by Wiggett Chute in the nineteenth century, and it is tempting to think that Chute may have placed another rococo ceiling here with Gothic elements suitable to the age of the panelling. A similar appli-

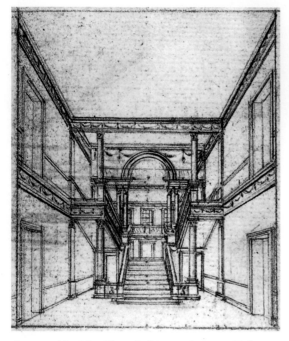

A proposal by John Chute for his new Staircase Hall

cation of blue paint to Jacobean panelling, with rosettes rather than stars, and with a rococo-Gothic ceiling survives in the Blue Parlour at Croft Castle.

The Chapel excited the Walpole group most of all because it encouraged their indulgence in quasi-Catholic ritual and dressing-up. When Walpole came to The Vyne late in 1754, he wrote to Richard Bentley, 'I carried down incense and mass books and we had a most Catholic enjoyment of the Chapel.' An ante-chapel clearly already existed when Walpole drew up his *Inventionary* in 1755, as he suggested that it should be 'finished as the end is' with armorial glass in the windows. What Chute added here was a thin fretwork of battens to the walls, with gold studs at the intersections, similar to that in the passage behind the Holbein Chamber at Strawberry Hill; clearly this pattern evoked a particular message of antiquity for Walpole's circle.

Walpole's main concern for the Chapel itself was to add pictures, part of the pseudo-Catholicising that he favoured. One of the works secured, *The Last Supper* by Giovanni Domenico Ferretti, now hangs in the Ante-Chapel. Also in that room is a painting which records the original arrangement of

the illusionistic canvases that Chute commissioned from the artist Spiridione Roma for the upper part of the south wall of the Chapel, and for which the latter was paid the huge sum of £360 13s in 1771. In the nineteenth century the canvases were moved to the Chapel Gallery, and the National Trust restored the scheme in 1998–9.

For Chute the period of the house that was perhaps of the greatest significance was the mid-seventeenth century. His full imagination was brought to bear on two projects that paid tribute to that time: the central staircase and the tomb chamber off the chapel. In the 1754 inventory, the central space is described as the 'Stone Hall and Stairs'. This space was probably divided into two floors to permit access from one side of the house to the other at both levels, and this access Chute had to maintain as he thought of a variety of ideas for halls and staircases. Among many drawings in his hand are some for vaulted Gothic halls and others that mix the classical with modern fashions, particularly one for a staircase with a Chinese-Gothic banister. Yet, just as in his detailed ideas for the centre of the south front, he usually abandoned the generalised Gothic style and got down to monumental solutions in the classical style, he always brought the staircase back to a classical solution because it matched the dignity of the Webb portico on the north front. The staircase, completed in 1770, also pays respect to the Webb period in its details of mouldings, balusters and the coffering of the ceiling. The mid-seventeenth-century staircase at Ashburnham House in Dean's Yard, Westminster, has been suggested as a prototype, which he would have known through the plan and section in Isaac Ware's *Designs of Inigo Jones*, published about 1733. It was Walpole who first used the word 'theatric' of the staircase, paying tribute to the illusionistic grandeur it lends to an awkwardly narrow space.

Chute undoubtedly got the idea for a family chapel, or 'columbarium', as he called it, from the sixteenth-century guild chapel of the Holy Trinity, commissioned by the 1st Lord Sandys at the Chapel of the Holy Ghost in Basingstoke. It was also conceived as a tomb chamber, though the great tomb chest at the centre was but a memorial to Chaloner Chute, whose remains were to stay at Chiswick.

The first idea had been simple: Richard Bentley designed three Gothic niches with urns to be inserted into the south wall of the Chapel itself. Chute himself then envisaged a separate structure, and two key drawings show his designs for the exterior and plan and the wall elevations of the interior. The careful detailing of the Gothic panelling and plaster ceiling is meant to evoke the rich decoration of late medieval chantry chapels; when the project began in the 1750s, Chute was looking at details of St George's Chapel, Windsor. Chute commissioned Edward Carter, a celebrated sculptor of marble fireplaces who had worked for Walpole, to complete what is one of the greatest late eighteenth-century monuments in England. Like the staircase, it is a free interpretation of the principles and architectural details of the mid-seventeenth century.

Both the effigy of the Speaker and the window of *The Adoration of the Magi* by John Rowell are taken from works attributed at this time to Van Dyck, again emphasising the importance of suitable period sources for the new work.

Chute died at his London house in 1776 before the tomb chamber was complete and it was left to his heir, his cousin Thomas Lobb, who assumed the name of Chute, to settle Carter's bill for almost £1,000. Chute's will, drawn up in 1774, left £300 to the poor of Sherborne St John. The day after Chute's death, Walpole wrote a long letter to Sir Horace Mann, once an intimate of the Strawberry circle that had somewhat drifted apart by this time: 'He was my counsel in affairs, was my oracle in taste, the standard to whom I submitted my trifles, and the genius that presided over poor Strawberry.'

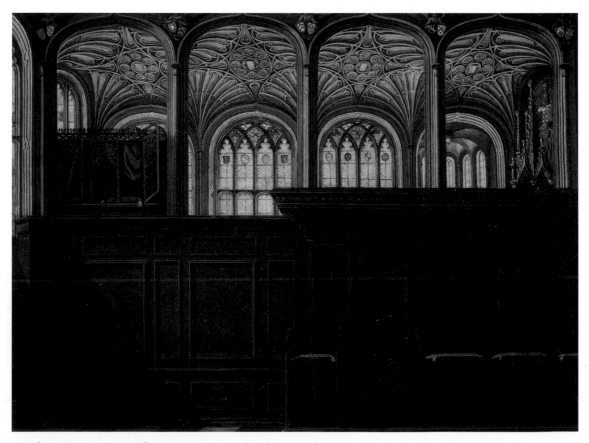

Spiridione Roma's proposal for the Gothic trompe-l'oeil painting for the south wall above the Chapel choir stalls

DECAY AND RECOVERY
THE NINETEENTH AND TWENTIETH
CENTURIES

A half-century of quiet neglect followed John Chute's death. *The Topographer* of 1789 opens by evoking a house as if from a fairy tale or romantic novel: '...the low, enclosed and wooded village of Sherborne ... thence the road lies up a winding lane ... some iron gates on the left unexpectedly open to the house' and it goes on to list old pictures, the Oak Gallery's panelling and the Chapel's stained glass as revered antiquities. The owners retreated into those few comfortable rooms they could keep warm, as the house became increasingly damp, and other areas, especially at the extreme ends where the

William John Chute; by Emma Smith
(South Bedroom)

chapel and gallery stood, became lumber rooms or were hardly used.

Chute's heir, Thomas Lobb, adopted the name of Chute on his inheritance. He completed the work on the Tomb Chamber (though he refused the new marble fireplace Chute had commissioned from Carter for the Drawing Room), and put in the screen which separates it from the Chapel. His son, William John Chute, owned the house from 1790 until 1824. He was MP for Hampshire for all but one year from 1790 to 1820. In the Commons he gained a reputation as an Independent, though he invariably supported William Pitt. Palmerston later described him as an 'hospitable squire' who 'preferred entertaining his neighbours at The Vyne to mixing with much zeal in parliamentary disputes'.

William John Chute founded the Vyne Hunt and was its Master until his death. The Hunt was organised rather chaotically, meets were seldom advertised and the hounds roamed at will in the gardens; in 1792 one litter was bred in a drain under the Drawing Room. J. F. R. Hope, the historian of hunting in Hampshire, recounts that William Chute 'was not fond of jumping but preferred to dismount in good time and, catching his horse by the tail, allowed the horse to pull him over an obstacle'. A sense of a benign but rather old-fashioned character is underlined in William Wigget Chute's comment that 'He was one of the last to wear a pigtail, and this hung by only a few hairs. His brother Thomas used to call it jokingly "his entailed Property (tie)".'

The Vyne was not without aristocratic connections at this period. The Duke of Wellington, who took up residence at Stratfield Saye in 1817, was a regular guest. William Chute's wife, Elizabeth Smith, was the sister of the Marchioness of Northampton and every couple of years the inner household of the Chutes and their personal servants would remove to Castle Ashby, her brother-in-law's Northamptonshire seat. We know something of the life and declining state of The Vyne in the early nineteenth century, thanks to the reminiscences of Caroline Wiggett, written in her old age in the 1860s. In 1803, the Chutes, still childless after ten years of marriage, took under their care the three-year-old Caroline, a second cousin to William's mother. They became known to her as 'aunt' and 'uncle'. She was therefore, as has recently been pointed out, a real-life Fanny Price, the poor relation heroine of Jane Austen's *Mansfield Park*. The connection with Jane Austen was not entirely literary, however, for her father and brothers frequently came to The Vyne at this time from the rectory of Steventon, a few miles away.

Caroline Wiggett was possibly the first child of the family to live at the house for a century. She records a quiet and rather lonely time with only the occasional child companion and long separation from her brothers and sisters. William and Elizabeth Chute moved between The Vyne and their London house as parliamentary duties required, but fashionable London society was rarely invited to Hampshire – one reason why so much of the house was left unmodernised. The house Caroline describes is a sad and dilapidated one. In her early years she slept in her aunt's unheated bedroom, probably the tower room over the Dining Parlour, terrified of the figures in the Soho tapestries, now in the Tapestry Room, which hung there on the bed and walls. The Tapestry Room became her aunt's and uncle's morning-room, and the Oak Gallery her own playroom, with a rocking horse at the far end. She describes it as 'a mere lumber room, a large gate-table in the middle, a common deal flooring, two or three cabinets, beautiful as they were, were not appreciated'. The Ante-Chapel was used to store coal and wood, while the Chapel itself was hardly ever entered.

Life was not all gloom. The Staircase Hall was redecorated, and Caroline records with great affection the social occasions that brought the community together. These included the half-yearly audit when the tenants dined in the steward's room, and the shop held annually at Michaelmas in the Dining Parlour (a room otherwise rarely used), which lasted a week and brought in for sale all kinds of

unmade cloth from Basingstoke. She helped her aunt assemble and paste prints on to canvas and then to the walls of the Print Room in about 1815, a fashionable mode of decoration at the period, which was also taken up at Stratfield Saye. William Chute used this room as his business office during the day. In July 1820 Caroline came of age; long tables were set up in the avenue approaching the house and she took tea with tenants' wives and daughters in the Starred Parlour (now the Saloon). She also records movingly Elizabeth Chute's care for the local community. Elizabeth founded the Sunday School, where Caroline taught from the age of twelve, and distributed food to the poor: 'Aunt C also every year gave away broth for the 3 winter months, which was made in a very large copper in the larder, at which she always presided at 8 o'clock in the morning ... in short an immense deal was given away.'

After William Chute's death in 1824, and that of his unmarried brother, Thomas, in 1827, Caroline continued to live at The Vyne with her widowed aunt until 1837, when she married a local surgeon, Thomas Workman. By this time, her brother, William Lyde Wiggett, had inherited the house but was yet to live there. His arrival on Elizabeth Chute's death in 1842 was to usher in a period of great change.

William Lyde Wiggett, was the chosen heir of the brothers William and Thomas Chute and he took the family name upon his succession in 1827. He had studied at Oxford and been called to the Bar at Middle Temple. Before inheriting The Vyne he had lived at another Chute house, Pickenham Hall in Norfolk, which he commissioned the architect W.J. Donthorne to rebuild. Wiggett Chute, as he came to be known, sold the Pickenham estate in 1842, which enabled him to carry out much-needed improvements and repairs. He finally cut his ties with East Anglia in 1847 by relinquishing his seat as MP for West Norfolk.

Wiggett Chute's work on the house is recorded in his *Reminiscences* and his accounts, and in the testimony of his son, Chaloner, who gathered together all the surviving evidence of his father's work. Wiggett Chute began by reorganising the estate, (see p. 40). Between 1842 and 1847 he spent £12,654 9s on the fabric of the house and a further

The south front in 1866, after the central porch had been added; by Elizabeth Chute

£2,647 16s 9d on furnishings. Much of this was spent on consolidation, for, improver though he was, he retained the historic integrity of the house.

Wiggett Chute first improved the house's immediate surroundings. By removing many tons of earth from the south front, he lowered the ground by five feet, thus relieving the previous impression that the house lay in a hollow, with two steps down into it on the south side. In front of the north façade, he created the gravel terrace walk where previously grass had come up to the very front of the house.

His alterations to the exterior were modest, alleviating its 'plainness', as he put it. He removed the gables from the east and west wings and created the present south-facing bay windows. He later took down the top of the square tower at the centre of the south front, which had been added by John Chute in the eighteenth century, and replaced it with a gable, in the belief that he was restoring the façade's original appearance. He also re-roofed the house and removed a two-feet thick covering of ivy from the south front. This provoked criticism from those who believed ivy was associated with the Romans and therefore appropriate to a site supposedly Roman in origin. With his characteristic good sense, Wiggett Chute countered that the passion for ivy was a very recent phenomenon. On the west side he added a porch to the entry to the Stone Gallery. On the north he added two blind Gothic windows to the north wall of the Chapel, removing the screen of trees that had stood here since the

eighteenth century, and put up battlements on the ranges flanking the portico to match those of the Chapel wing.

His changes to the historic rooms were equally respectful, although he did move fireplaces and doors around, and rearrange the sixteenth-century tiles in front of the choir-stalls, and move the Spiridione Roma canvases to their present position. He must also have been responsible for the present ceiling of the Chapel, since the wooden ribs are shown in a different arrangement over the east end in the drawing of 1812. He bought a few items at the great Strawberry Hill sale of 1842 including the miniature after Batoni of John Chute and an oval portrait by Müntz, clearly for the value of their associations. Sadly, a large quantity of china also purchased from Strawberry Hill was found to be broken on arrival. He noted carefully the sources of purchases with aristocratic or royal connections: an ormolu ebony table formerly belonged to the Duke of Cambridge, son of George III, a sculpture of the infant Bacchus came from Lady Blessington, and a dining-table and silk curtains were purchased from the Marquess of Winchester. He rescued the Ante-Chapel from its fate as a coal and wood store and cleared the Oak Gallery of its accumulations of books and prints piled on sofas. He regretted that the repair of the woodwork in the Gallery was not better done; his son Chaloner was to seek ways of removing the paint in 1881.

The Library represents most fully Wiggett Chute's attempt to create an historic interior in keeping with the house. He installed the bookcases, their cornice coming from the Vyne pew in Sherborne church, and he brought the ceiling ribs out of the North Bedroom, which he largely dismantled. He bought eight carved chairs (in Carolean style to match the portraits gathered here) for £30, the library table for 8 guineas and the ten plaster busts of famous classical and native writers for £14 the set.

However, Wiggett Chute's main concern was to make The Vyne a modern family home. He brought running water to the upper floors for the first time and extended the water supply to the stables and other outbuildings. The drains under the house were a mystery, so he sent a boy down into them, noting that 'at one time to the alarm of all others as well as himself he was lost for some hours but fortunately no harm happened to him and all the drains were mapped'. In the east wing Wiggett Chute made provision for a large household of children and servants, adding sixteen new bedrooms and moving the servants' hall. He was also anxious to do away with the previous informal arrangement of rooms opening off each other and masters and mistresses sleeping close to their servants' bedrooms. He built a new back stairs 'nearer the Hall which is better for the family use' and made the passage above the kitchen, 'giving access to all the rooms without making any a thoroughfare as before'. In his own way he was reproducing the complex system of passages and stairs that were designed to keep owners and servants apart in the purpose-built Victorian country house.

The family life of the house is captured in the series of watercolours by Wiggett Chute's wife, Martha, and their daughter, Elizabeth, painted in the 1850s and 1860s. They are a remarkable record of the mixture of new and old furniture; eighteenth-century cabinets and side-tables, mirrors and sconces stand alongside newly purchased rosewood central tables, banquettes and sofas.

Chaloner Chute inherited The Vyne in 1879, and nine years later published his *History of The Vyne*, for which he had long been assembling material. At his death in 1892, he was succeeded by his son, Charles, who became a baronet in 1952. During his long tenure the present drive was created to the south of the house in 1911–12, electric light installed in 1920, and numerous repairs made, including the re-leading of the Chapel windows. Sir Charles also made many invaluable notes on the history of the house.

Chaloner William and Eleanor Chute and their children, about 1888

After 1919 the Chutes reduced the size of their estate and in 1920 let The Vyne to Lucie James, an Australian educationalist who turned the house into a girls' boarding school. The family returned in 1930, but during the Second World War The Vyne again became a school, when a prep school from Deal in Kent was evacuated here, thanks to a promise made by Sir Charles to its headmaster, F. G. Turner, with whom he had served in the First World War. During recent repair work, children's drawings were discovered under the floorboards. The family remained in the house, happily coexisting with their young guests. At Sir Charles's death in 1956, he bequeathed The Vyne, its contents and the estate of 1,124 acres, with an endowment, to the National Trust. Lady Chute, who, with great generosity, had forgone her many rights to the property, went to live in a smaller house on the estate.

BIBLIOGRAPHY

MANUSCRIPT SOURCES

Among the few manuscripts still at the house are Caroline Wiggett Workman's *Account of The Vyne as it was in bygone days* and William Wiggett Chute's *History of the Vyne House and Property*, compiled in 1872 and his expenditure accounts for the 1840s. The Chute family papers are in the Hampshire Record Office; these include medieval deeds, accounts for building in the 1650s, accounts for purchases of furniture by Anthony Chute, the inventories of 1754, 1776 and 1842, the majority of John Chute's drawings for the house, William Wiggett Chute's *Reminiscences*, Chaloner Chute's notebook with earlier documents and drawings pasted therein, and notes by Sir Charles Chute on the history of the house. Other drawings by John Chute for The Vyne are in one of his sketchbooks, now in the Lewis Walpole Library, Farmington, Connecticut, USA. The 1541 inventory of the house is among the Duke of Rutland's family papers at Belvoir Castle, Leicestershire.

ANON., 'History of The Vyne', *The Topographer*, ii, May 1789.

BEHARRELL, C. H., 'Comfortable Ensemble: A Victorian and his Family at The Vyne', *Country Life*, clxxv, 1984, pp. 476–7.

BOLD, John, *John Webb: Architectural Theory and Practice in the Seventeenth Century*, Oxford, 1989.

CHARLESTON, R. J., 'Souvenirs of the Grand Tour', *Journal of Glass Studies*, i, 1959, pp. 62–81.

CHUTE, Chaloner W., *A History of The Vyne in Hampshire*, Winchester, 1888.

CHUTE, Sir Charles L., 'A Monument by Thomas Carter', *Country Life*, 27 May 1954, pp. 1733–4.

CLIMENSON, Emily J., ed., *Passages from the Diaries of Mrs Philip Lybbe Powys*, London, 1899, pp. 203–4.

COLERIDGE, Anthony, 'Eighteenth-Century Furniture at The Vyne', *Country Life*, 25 July 1963, pp. 214–16.

CORNFORTH, John, 'Breath of Italy', *Country Life*, 30 March 1989, pp. 106–7.

HARRISSON, W. D., and Viscount Chandos, *Carvings: Oak Gallery, The Vyne, Hampshire*, Sherborne St John, 1979.

HOWARD, Maurice, *The Early Tudor Country House: Architecture and Politics 1490–1550*, London, 1987.

HYMERSMA, Herbert-Jan, 'Guido di Savino and other Antwerp potters of the sixteenth century', *Connoisseur*, August 1977.

LELAND, John, *Itinerary*, ed. L. Toulmin-Smith, London, 1906–8, ii, p. 8.

LUMMIS, Trevor, and Jan Marsh, *The Woman's Domain: Women and the English Country House*, London, 1990, pp. 91–118.

McCARTHY, Michael, 'John Chute's Drawings for The Vyne', *National Trust Yearbook*, 1975–6, pp. 70–80, and *The Origins of the Gothic Revival*, New Haven and London, 1987.

McLEOD, Bet, 'Horace Walpole and Sèvres porcelain', *Apollo*, January 1998, pp. 42–7.

NARES, Gordon, 'The Vyne, Hampshire', *Country Life*, 3 January 1957, pp. 16–19.

RUSHFORTH, G. McN., 'The Painted Windows in the Chapel of The Vyne', and 'The Origin of the Windows in the Chapel of The Vyne in Hampshire', *Walpole Society*, xv, 1926, pp. 1–20; xxv, 1936–7, pp. 167–9.

SMITH, W. H., *Originals Abroad*, New Haven, 1952 [pp. 157–76 on John Chute].

TIPPING, H. Avray, 'The Vyne, Hampshire', *Country Life*, 14, 21, 28 May 1921, pp. 582–9, 612–19, 642–9, and in *English Homes*, period II, i, 1924, pp. 93–116.

'Furniture at The Vyne', *Country Life*, 21, 28 May 1921, pp. 619–21, 649–51.

TRACY, Charles, *English Gothic Choir-Stalls 1400–1540*, Woodbridge, 1990.

The Victoria County History: Hampshire, iv, London, 1911, pp. 160–4.

WAINWRIGHT, Clive, *The Romantic Interior*, New Haven and London, 1989 [chapter 4 on Strawberry Hill].

Warner's Collections for the History of Hampshire and the Bishopric of Winchester, I [1795?], pp. 207–11.

WAYMENT, Hilary, 'The Stained Glass in the Chapel of The Vyne', *National Trust Studies*, London, 1980, pp. 35–48, and 'The Stained Glass of the Chapel of the Vyne and the Chapel of the Holy Ghost, Basingstoke', *Archaeologia*, cvii, 1982, pp. 141–52.

WORSLEY, Giles, 'The Vyne, Hampshire', *Country Life*, 9 May 1991, pp. 78–81.